The Empath ...

and Bach Flower Remedies for Empaths

A guide written for empaths, by an empath, for the new and advanced Empath.

Updated for 2018

By Gary R Leigh

If this book resonates with you, feel free to pass it along to someone else.

ISBN-13: 978-1507744505
ISBN-10: 1507744501

Other works and websites:

Bach Flower Remedies Questions, Answers and Support: https://www.facebook.com/groups/BFRHelp/

Empath Social: https://empathsupport.net/

Empath and psychic support blog:
https://psychicsupport.net

Books:
I am The Phoenix

The autobiography of Gary R. Leigh.
Think a phoenix is a myth? Well, think again.

You can find more information on empaths and other related material at empathsupport.net

Who am I?

Hi, my name is Gary and I'm an Empath.

I'm also a student of Bach Flower Remedies. I have been researching and studying them intensely since 1994. Much of my study is on how these remedies can help others, especially the Empath. I have made many discoveries and insights into how the remedies work. These are important and I have shared them in this book.

I have also run many support groups, websites and blogs for Empaths since 2005.

I am a certified life coach and extremely intuitive when it comes to helping and healing others.

I have helped and healed thousands of people over the years. I consider it my calling.

I have experienced more psychic events than I can remember and I have studied long and hard to obtain the level of knowledge and attunement to energies I now have.

This book has been written with the Empath in mind. I believe it takes an Empath to help one and I feel this work will certainly do this.

I hope you enjoy this book and what it has to offer.

Part 1 – Being an Empath.

Preface

Are you an Empath? Someone who picks up on other people's feelings? You may well be one and not know it.

Every day, more people are discovering that there is nothing wrong with them and the feelings they have had all their lives are normal.

They are not oversensitive.

They are not crazy after all!

In this book we look at:

- The Signs of being an Empath
- What to be aware of.
- What to do about it
- How to protect yourself
- And how to use Bach Flower Remedies to help live a happier, fuller life.
- How others can influence you with their energies
- Psychic attacks and what to do about them.
- And much, much more.

It's been my intention to write a book on being an Empath for a number of years. However, it's been pretty hard to get started on it.

Eventually, I decided to ask the help of my guides. I have used this method before with good results. The format takes on a "Conversation with God" type format: Not as a template, but out of necessity, as I don't see any other way to write this kind of book.

The way I wrote it was to ask the questions, and let my guide answer through me. I never knew quite what would come out, and often it was not what I was expecting.

Hopefully you will find it as engaging to read as it was for me to write.

Just in case anyone is wondering, I don't do drugs, drink, or seek out controversial cults, etc. This was written as pure channelling. I'll leave the results for you to decide if it's useful information or not.

Just a note on how I channel. When I'm writing something, I can sense that my guide wants to come through, so I will open myself up to the answers.

Most of the time, I have no clue what I'm going to get, and am curious myself about what the answer could be for some of the questions.

I also don't remember what has been written until I reread it later.

I know who my guide is, but I feel that revealing the name will be only a distraction here.

This book launches right into the conversation without any preamble.

Some of the subject matter will be considered controversial, but it appears to have come up as certain aspects of being an empath were being discussed. Much of it is esoteric in nature and I invite you to check if it resonates with you as some of it can be quite challenging to the belief system.

As with anything, take what works, leave the rest, and always go by what feels right for you.

Each section has a summary of the main points, in case people are trying to find something quickly, which I also put at the end of the book.

The second part of this book focuses on the Bach Flower Remedies. I refer to them a lot because I've seen amazing results with them, and I really believe they should be in the tool kit of every empath.

Enjoy.

Signs of Being an Empath

Okay, where do we start?

The Empath's guidebook, as the title suggests, is a book for empaths. It is for those who are looking for information and for those who are taking their first few faltering steps into the world of being an empath.

Let's begin with typical signs that one is an empath. I won't say symptoms because that seems to indicate that something is wrong, whereas being an empath is actually a natural state of being.

Okay, so what are some of the signs of being an empath?

As the name suggests, an empath is one who can feel and pick up on the emotions and feelings of others around them. That is the basic premise, though it is very much more than that. An empath is often psychic on many levels, too.

You might suggest that being empathic is akin to being psychic, and you could successfully argue that, but it's only so in the strict definition of the word. We are all psychic and empathic, though many have chosen to disconnect from that ability in order to experience what it is like not to be one with all that is.

There is a growing number of people where this is no longer the case. We are reaching an age where empaths are more common than not, and many more will begin to awaken as well. We are approaching a period in our history in which many may refer to as 'The Age of the Empath'.

So, you, who are reading this, may well ask: Am I an empath?

How do I know I'm just not crazy? How can I tell if I am not being delusional here? Aren't empaths the stuff of science fiction?

And those are good questions that should be asked because it's unwise to take anything on faith, as what we often put our faith into is not always what our truths are.

First, let me assure you that not only are empaths real, but there are a growing number of people who are discovering that they are empaths themselves.

There are many signs that one may be empathic. It's more than just picking up on the feelings of others, much, much more.

Let us look at some of the signs.

A major one is loss of your sense of self.

This is when you don't know where you end emotionally and others begin. The empath will typically take on the fear and pain of others and make it their own. They hear a sad tale, and empathize with it, feeling that somehow there is strength in solidarity.

They notice someone in pain, and they wish to make them feel better. Their heart goes out to the person and they feel bad for them.

They read, hear, and see all the terrible and insane events of this world and feel obliged to feel bad about it.

All the while, they are literally absorbing the psychic energies from others. They are a psychic sponge and that means they absorb so much psychic pollution that they become clogged with it.

To give an analogy, it's like a very absorbent sponge that you have used to mop up numerous spills but have not taken the trouble to cleanse. Should you squeeze its heavy-laden content, you'll most likely find a thick, unpleasant, foul liquid flow out from it.

To be around such people is not that pleasant either, as any normal empath will sense something is wrong, and a highly attuned empath won't even be able to approach them from any distance.

In the meantime, the empaths themselves will be feeling more and more distressed and depressed as time goes on and may often feel they are going mad. Every day is a challenge to them, and every moment is full of weariness, as all they experience is more of the same with no hope and no end in sight. Many even become suicidal.

If the empath happens to also be psychic in some way, that can compound the problem. The telepath will not only be picking up the emotions from all around them, but they will also pick up thoughts from people and entities that are drawn to them.

Such beings often attack on a psychic level, and feed off the misery of others. Are they dangerous to one's health? Very much so.

So, what exactly are entities?

Disembodied spirits. They are soul aspects, or if you wish, souls, who exist on another level. Some would claim not to have a soul, but we are all made of the same stuff.

This is said to be the third dimensional level (or 3D as some call it), and all that you can touch, feel, hear, smell, detect is considered to be part of it.

Anything that's on another vibrational level could be said to be in the astral levels. The astral is simply any other level that isn't of this level. It can be higher vibration or lower, and it's relative to where you are.

To those on a higher astral level, the 3D would be considered a lower astral level.

On the astral levels, things may be as solid as they are in the 3D, because everything is proportionate to the speed of the vibrations.

You mean, if something vibrates extremely fast, everything else around it vibrates at a similar speed and gives the illusion of being solid?

Yes. Even on this level, it's acknowledged that so-called solid objects are mostly space.

The thing with this particular level is that our soul aspects, which are the aspects of the one soul, inhabit a body.

Entities that are disembodied are in spirit form. They use no body and aren't bound by the same rules as you are in the third dimension.

Beings such as this can see and do things that are considered to be supernatural, and they can move at the speed of thought.

Such beings exist on all levels. We are surrounded by them all the time, and while many work for the good of us, there are some that don't. They are the ones who can cause the empath much distress.

So, would you be suggesting ghosts, demons, or other such things?

Remember, everything exists on some level. Demons, demonics, nature spirits, the so called otherkin (who are non human spirits who sometimes inhabit human bodies) and much, much more. They are real, even if you can't see them.

There is nothing that doesn't exist.

I'm sure there are a lot of people who don't believe in entities or spirits, let alone psychic attacks.

There are more things out there than you could believe. As I just said, everything exists on some level, and this is simply one of those things. Yes, entities that feed off negativity not only exist, but are everywhere, and all around us. But they are not evil, not in the truest sense; they are simply doing what they feel they must do to survive. The key is to not make yourself a meal for them. Such beings are victims of their own realities and there is little joy in them for they have forgotten their own connection and oneness to all.

So you're saying that something like a demon is misunderstood?

In the strictest sense, they are, but do not make the error of believing they need or want our understanding or our sympathy. Some enjoy being malicious. It's who they are and what their function is.

However, that is another topic. The point here is that the polluted empath is very vulnerable to them.

I'm curious, how do they feed? How does it work? If the empath is so vulnerable to these entities, how do they protect themselves, and isn't talking about such things going to freak some people out?

Well, yes, it may do so; however ignoring such things does not make them go away. Knowledge and understanding is the key to defending yourself against such beings. When you understand what you are up against, and how they operate, then it's much easier to deal with them.

But isn't discussing such things giving focus and energy to it? Doesn't that make it stronger?

It depends on what you are discussing and how. If you are coming from a place of fear, then yes, indeed, it can make them stronger. If you are coming from a place of light and love, then you are shedding light on the subject and revealing what is really happening.

Without getting into the metaphysics of it all, as that would take a chapter or two, suffice it to say that such beings are there to aid us in such a way that we know ourselves in the absence of who we really are. They are playing a part, and it's not an easy part, but someone has to play it in order for the other party to know who they really are.

This is who the beings are on the purest level. Therefore, do not condemn them, but rather bless them.

That being said, you do not need to be used as a source for their energy. In fact, by falling into such situations, you are doing both parties a great disservice, unless it is your intention to go down that particular path, in which case, that's another choice you are making.

So yes, dark and negative entities do exist, but only as a relative term. It may be of interest that to others, they would appear as beings as light, and to extremely high-level beings, they would appear as the darker ones. It is relative.

Thus, do not condemn that which you fear or do not understand.

Okay, so we've established that these being are not evil, and that they are victims themselves, so how do they actually operate? How do they actually feed?

I would not use the word 'victims'. They are more aptly described as a product of their own created reality, (and some would no doubt dispute this) but that point aside, they feed on energy.

All life feeds on energy in its own way. We gain energy through air, food, chi, prana, nature, our own source, other people, animals, minerals, and many other sources. Food is actually our main source of gaining energy, though, it should be stated that it's not the only source.

There have been people who have not only fed off the energies of the universe, but thrived from it. It should be noted, though, that the human body was not designed to just sustain itself on such energies. To do so makes it untethered from this reality and makes it hard for the person to remain here as they tend to shift to higher vibrational levels, and thus, higher astral levels.

In order for us to function properly on the third dimension, as we call it, we must ingest food sources from that level. The energy we take in is what helps ground and sustain us. Unfortunately, much of the food around today is not good for us. It lacks the healthy energy that we need to remain healthy. A piece of fruit might look appealing and large, but a sensitive person can tell there is little or no energy contained within it.

Entities, which are often disembodied spirits, that is, spirits that have not taken on a physical form in the third dimension, or 3D as some refer to it as, have their own food source. Like anything else, they are seeking a way to grow and become stronger.

As a rule, they seek energy that is similar to themselves in order to feed upon. If a being is considered dark, their natural preference is for energy that is dark. They will then seek out someone who will emit that kind of energy and feed off it.

One of the techniques they constantly use is to create situations that will enable such energy to be created. There are many types of entities wishing to feed, and so there are many different types of scenarios that may be created.

For example, the entity will send dark thoughts to the target's mind, telling them awful things

to try and make them fall into a dark depression. The target will hear in their mind, thoughts about how everyone is better off without them, and how destroying themselves or taking themselves away from their loved ones is the kindest thing they can do.

To the target, it sounds seductive and makes perfect sense. They focus on the things they consider flaws within themselves and feel that they are holding others back. People have committed suicide due to this, which brings about a massive release of negative energies, not only from the person who dies, but also from the loved ones around them. The entity then gets its fill, at least for a little while.

But such energy does not sate or satisfy it for long. It will gain nothing that will aid it, except a longing for more energy. It's very much like eating fast food as your only diet. You feel good for a very short while, but you become sicker and more depressed as time goes on.

Such dark energies are easy to spot for someone who is sensitive. If you relax your eyes and look from your third eye, the room will become dark, as though it is covered in a cloud. If you look at someone's face, it will fade into darkness, as though a dark shadow is upon it.

Sending light and thoughts of love to the darkness will clear it very quickly, and the person who is affected will recover very quickly as the shadows clear.

It's fair to say that while many depressed people are the target of such entities, they also target what you would term 'light-workers'.

You might ask why bother, as such beings are not compatible with the energies they seek. The reason is that light-workers are considered a threat to the food source. If the entity can bring them into a state of depression and darkness, not only do they have another source to feed off, but they have also stopped what they perceive to be a threat to their own existence and growth.

Generally, sending thoughts of love and warmth and light will repel such energies. Often people will tell you to surround yourself in a bubble of white light, however, that is actually not all that helpful. White light, without being filled with love and warmth is empty light. You might as well turn on the kitchen light for the same token.

When you surround yourself with light, visualize the colours that bring comfort and joy to you. Act with love and joy in mind. Make it part of your being. Make it part of your shield. Send it to those who are dark around you and bless them. Love, warmth, and joy are tremendous healers, though be aware that the result is often that you will chase away the darkness, rather than heal it.

With that being said, it's also very important that you never attack the darkness back.

Yes, that is something that should be made very clear. If you try to attack or destroy a negative entity, you will just make it stronger as you are feeding it the energy it desires. You are actually making things worse for all concerned, especially yourself.

You cannot change energy by feeding it more of the same. There are those who will get all 'gung-ho' and believe they are spiritual defenders, or warriors, and that it is their duty to destroy all the darkness.

The irony is that, not only do they not heal anything, but they also become what they have judged and condemned. Light will never attack. It will always find a way through love.

Um… I disagree. Light sometimes does attack. Look at the Archangels. Well, at least, the ones who have humanities interests at heart.

Let us define attack then. It means to take on another party and reduce them so they are no longer a perceived threat. The threat may be anything you deem to be against your own vested interests.

Light will defend. Light will work to protect. Light will give people the tools they need to help survive their own attacks. Light will inspire, energize, and bring love and hope. Light will remove the source of the attack, possibly taking it to a place where it no longer can hurt others. But Light will never attack to destroy or diminish. If they did, they would become part of the problem, and no longer be the Light-worker they aspire to be.

Whatever Light does, it does from a place of compassion and love.

It is not actually possible to destroy any entity or being or soul. They will always return at some point to plague you until such times you have either come to a resolution, or a soul agreement, or one of the parties has moved beyond the reach of the other.

Any soul, no matter who they are, would do well to bless and heal their attackers. By doing this, you are healing yourself, putting out energies to stop the attacks, and ultimately healing everyone.

Just imagine if people sent love to those they hate and fear instead of sending men and arms. This world could change overnight.

Okay, I get that. What I don't get here is why we're discussing it so early on. How is this a sign of being an empath?

It's important on two levels.

The first is that many empaths are being attacked by such entities, and they need to understand what is happening to them.

The second is that it's a sign that you are an empath, as empaths are typically targeted, as they tend to be much more vulnerable than non-empathic people. It's also one of the reasons why many empaths suffer from clinical depression.

Empathy, while in the negative, can be considered a curse and there are many an empath who wish this 'gift' would be taken away from them.

This guide will look into how to shift the curse into a blessing and how to use the empathic abilities in a positive and life affirming way.

Summary

- An empath can lose their sense of self in other people, world events, or strong energies.
- They may absorb negative energies like sponge absorbs water and dirt.
- Astral entities may feed of the negative energy of the empath.
- Sending thoughts of love, joy, and light helps protect you against such beings.

Sensitivity to Light, Noise and Smells

Okay, so far, the signs we have are loss of sense of self and psychic attacks by entities. What else is there?

> *Well, you've actually made a long list of signs, and we should go through them one by one and add others as we come to them.*
>
> *The first on your list is: sensitivity to light and noise.*
>
> *This is actually something that non-empaths may experience, too, so just because you have such experiences, it does not automatically mean you are an empath.*
>
> *Empaths typically experience such sensitivities when they are exhausted and feeling very ungrounded. Their soul tends to expand beyond their body, in order to try and keep the body functioning. When that occurs, the energies around them tend to impact them on a greater level. It's like leaving a darkened room and walking into bright light. It takes a while to adjust.*
>
> *This is a warning sign of exhaustion, something that the empath is prone to, and should be taken seriously. Rest and down time is important here, though the empath doesn't always feel they can take it.*

I think we really need to define certain concepts here. If someone who is unfamiliar with spirituality reads this, they will be lost at such statements as their soul expanding beyond their body. What does it actually mean? I'm not sure what it means myself.

We could get into the nitty gritty of how this all works, but we will keep it at a simple level. It is generally accepted that we have a soul. That is the life-force within you and houses the body. The body does not contain the soul but rather the other way around, as the soul is simply an aspect of the larger whole, and it's not possible for it to be separate from its source.

The illusion is that the body contains the soul, and the soul aspect generally shrinks to accommodate the dimensions of the body. The etheric and the aura, which some can actually see, are the energies of the soul as it expands beyond the body.

If someone comes into that area where the soul expands beyond the body, they will feel it, and say that others are coming into their personal space. How big the area is depends on where they are and the number of other people around them.

Country people, who are more in tune with the land and nature, will have a much larger expansion of their personal space, as they not only need it to connect to their surroundings, but also there are fewer people around to intrude.

City people have learned to hold their energies in very close and so their own personal space is much smaller.

When the soul needs to expand itself past its normal boundaries, it will not be used to the extra energy and information coming at it.

Your next sign is that the empath is sensitive to harsh lights and strong smells, which may trigger strong feelings within them.

We've already covered the sensitivity to light, which, as I said, can also be a sign of exhaustion, amongst other things. Strong smells may well trigger emotions in anyone, such as music, movies, stories, and so forth. While it's true that some empaths may find this to be particularly strong, it is certainly not exclusive to empaths.

Some people can actually pick up on smells that aren't from the material world. They are sensitive enough to pick them up from astral beings.

Astral being defined as any vibrational level lower or higher than this current level, right?

Yes. Empaths might well smell odours that are either pleasant or unpleasant. It's not unusual to smell something that is foul or a pleasant fragrance with no discernible source. Often, they can be signs that energy vampires or loved ones may be around.

By energy vampires, you mean astral beings that feed of our energies, right?

Yes. You may refer to them as energy vampires because they feed off energies. Of course, such types of beings are not exclusive to just the astral levels. This world is full of them.

So what is the benefit of smelling astral smells?

It's simply a way to be aware that there is more than just you in the room. Actually, there is always more than you in the room, just not on the same astral levels. Some are just too fine to see, except in the mind's eye.

And the mind's eye is?

That place within your mind where you can visualize things.

Summary

- An empath is more sensitive to light and noise when they are exhausted.

- Their personal space will expand past their normal boundaries.
- They may also pick up smells from astral levels.
- Smells may indicate the presence of other beings being around you.

Sensitivity to Crowds and Parties

> *The next sign that one is an empath is that they find it hard to tolerate parties, nightclubs, overcrowded venues, or shopping plazas, to name just a few.*
>
> *How well they cope will often depend on who is around, how noisy it is, and what type of energies and substances are being consumed.*

I know that parties and me just never mixed. In my teens and twenties, I'd have to go to them, or go out with friends, and all I could do was look at my watch and try to last as long as I could without appearing impolite or a party pooper. As I don't drink, or do drugs, or smoke, and I couldn't stand the deafening music, it was quite a trial for me. At the time, I did not know I was an empath, and was oversensitive to such things. I could not, for the life of me, comprehend why people seemed to enjoy themselves so much when I could hardly bear it.

> *Being grounded is a large part of coping with such things. If you feel like an intruder, or that you do not belong, or that you don't fit in for whatever reason, you become ungrounded, which makes it much worse for you.*
>
> *When lacking confidence and assurance that you should be somewhere, you attempt to escape, and as you can't leave with your body,*

your spirit does the next best thing and attempts to move to a happier place.

Your body is there, but you are no longer fully present. This makes it hard to function in any setting.

The key to being grounded is self-confidence. If you believe you have the right to be somewhere, and it's somewhere you wish to be, you will become grounded. Even ungrounded people will become grounded when they are in their element.

We'll look at self-confidence later on.

How much people are affected depends on who they are, how much they wish to be somewhere, and how grounded they are feeling.

In an e-mail to you, it was pointed out that this person actually enjoyed going to shopping malls and experiencing the energies around them. If you are able to do such a thing, it is quite an interesting and healthy way to deal with being in crowds, provided you are able to remain self- confident to a reasonable extent.

Being ungrounded is neither good nor bad. It simply is a state of being. If it's how you wish to be, then that's fine. The problem is that many do not actually enjoy being that way.

When I first started on this particular part of this journey, I was told that the best way to become grounded was to do something physical, such as yoga, and I had to do it every day. I did that for a year, but I don't feel it helped me all that much.

I did certainly become more flexible, but I don't think that was the goal!

> *Depends on who you are. Physical stuff actually is very good, but if you don't wish to be doing it, or you don't want to be there, then it doesn't help you very much. A healthy body goes a long way to feeling good within, and that, in turn, helps ground people.*
>
> *It didn't help you all that much because you never solved the root issues you had during that time. Once you eventually did that, you were able to ground yourself naturally.*
>
> *The lesson to take from that experience is that only you really know what works for you. Others may think they have the answer, but they are simply other perspectives.*

Summary

- An empath may struggle to be comfortable if they don't feel they belong or fit in.
- One of the keys to being grounded is self-confidence.

- Physical activity can help ground you.

yoga
Woods walking

Anxiety

Okay, the next sign I wrote about is that you may experience anxiety for no apparent reason and you're not able to resolve it or get over it.

> *Yes, anxiety is the hardest thing on an empath. It normally has to do with vague fears and worries, and the sense that something is amiss, but you do not know what.*

> *There are many reasons for anxiety. Normally it's to do with a lack of faith that things will work out, a lack of faith in what you are doing, and a lack of faith in your own destiny. Those who suffer from clinical depression tend to suffer greatly from anxiety, and no matter what they try, they just can't get over it.*

Well, unless you're using the Bach Flower Remedy, Aspen, that is.

> *Aspen certainly does help, but the key is to find the root cause and deal with that.*

> *Now here's the problem. You have an empath who carries such deep anxieties within them, and the likelihood is that another empath will pick up on those feelings. Because they are vague and have no real definition, the second empath will then have a sense of foreboding or doom, which they cannot quite define or understand.*

> *If they can understand that it's not coming from them, it will go a long way to dealing with this. However some empaths are natural worriers, and if they are not focused on themselves, they are always worrying about another.*

I know that it drives me crazy when people worry about me. I don't really enjoy that kind of attention. It's as though they don't trust me enough to know that things are working out as they are meant to be.

> *Well, worry is fear. You tend to fear that something unpleasant will happen to someone you care about. It's also not very productive. Empaths are often worrying about others. Some might say that it's in their nature, but they can drive the target crazy with their incessant worrying.*

> *An empath who is attuned to another will naturally tend to pick up on the stress levels and anxiety that is occurring.*

I find that when I have a bad day, people tend to spam me with messages asking what is wrong and that makes things worse. I then have to console them and take focus away from my own healing and renewing of energies. The best thing they could do is either leave me alone, or say that they are sending healing thoughts my way.

This is certainly one of the best things you can do for someone. As a general rule, do not try to fix someone who has not asked to be fixed. They may not be broken in the first place. Most of the time, they know what they need to do, and the last thing they should be doing is entering into a discussion on what another feels they should be doing. If someone needs help, they will generally send out a soul call, which is a call for help on a soul level, and it will be answered.

The empath does not really know or understand all this, though. All they feel is that something is terribly wrong, and they can't explain the feelings they have.

In my experience, this can also lead to a vicious cycle if two empaths are picking up on each other. If one is having a bad day, and the other picks up on this and takes it as their own feelings. Then the other empath will pick up on those feelings, and take it as their own, and so on.

That certainly is one scenario. The general one, though, is that while one empath is stressing about something, the other will fear it's about something they have done. They will then have a feeling of guilt, fear, and anxiety, thinking about all the terrible things they may have (but never actually) have done.

The other empath then picks up on such things, and being unable to then focus on themselves, they find themselves very irritated and annoyed that they must first focus on healing the other before they can refocus on themselves.

As you said, it's a vicious cycle. It's the guilt part that really does the most damage. It's amazing just how many people will automatically assume that if someone is having a bad day, it's because it's something they have done.

Good communication is the key here. If you are having a bad day, simply say: I'm having a bad day. I'm not ready to discuss things yet, but don't worry, it's nothing to do with you. All I need is your understanding and support, and I'll be okay.

Yes, that can certainly help, though it's not always easy for someone to say that, especially if it happens on a consistent basis, and by that I mean, it seems to happen every other day.

Some do indeed feel that they are like a broken record, but that's just life. Things happen, sometimes on a daily basis. You should not need to apologize for it. Over time, you will put coping techniques into place, and you will know what you need to do to get back to your centre.

Well, the other problem is that we're also afraid of offending someone. Many people are easily offended, and they also can make your issues about themselves. Suddenly, it's no longer about you, and you have to put your own issues on hold while you deal with their dramas. So you'd rather not say anything to anyone in the first place, and hope they don't notice.

People can only choose to be offended. If it wasn't your intention to offend, then that is their issue, not yours.

Someone once said to me, you can't give offence, only take it.

True, and some willingly choose to be offended as they wish to generate the drama to feed off the energy, or have the focus upon them. Such things are referred to as control dramas, which are explained succinctly in the Celestine Prophecy, and people will use one form or another if they feel that they need the energy.

This is akin to those astral entities that feed off energy, and like the energy they feed off of, it's not healthy or productive, nor will it nourish or bring any joy or peace. It's like a fast food snack. It tastes great while you're eating it, but afterwards you really don't feel so good for it.

> *It's a good idea to surround yourself with people who will uplift and support you, though some people are harder to avoid than others. Family can be the hardest, and often people come to a choice where they have to decide to cut them out of their life, or put up with their antics. Families, especially parents, are experts at playing the guilt card.*
>
> *Once again, communicating what you are feeling, if you are able to, can help, but what is more important is knowing your boundaries, setting them, and sticking to them.*

Summary

- Empaths tend to feel anxious without knowing why.
- This may be due to a lack of faith that all is as it should be.
- They also may be picking up feelings from others.
- Worrying about another person can make them feel worried, too.
- If someone needs your help, you will feel their soul call.
- Good communication is important to stop empathic couples going into a downward spiral of drama and anxiety.
- Set your boundaries and stay within them.

And what are boundaries?

> *They are a set of limits that you will not go past, nor allow others to intrude upon. What they are is up to you, but if you decide that you are not going to be drawn into a negative drama, then that is a boundary, and you should be aware of that, and enforce it.*
>
> *People love to push others' boundaries and push their buttons to get reactions. Also being aware of your own buttons, which you might also call triggers, is important. People use these things to manipulate others to get what they want.*
>
> *Triggers can come from childhood traumas, bad experiences, or persecution, to name some examples. Some people are very giving, and thus their trigger is the need to help another and that is played upon by the other party.*
>
> *That is why you should think about who you are, what you wish to do, and how you wish to do it. With that knowledge, define your boundaries and do not allow others to get past them.*
>
> *Ask yourself, does this really need to be done right now? Often the answer is no, and if there*

is a genuine need to help another, then do so, as long as you are able to.

For some, there is always some emergency going on, though.

Yes, and those people feed into their own drama by allowing it to happen and creating the circumstances for it time and time again. Indulging them and helping them over and over again is actually unhealthy and unhelpful for both parties.

You can only really help another when they have decided to heal a situation, and they have asked for help in doing so. It's a sad truth that many actually do not wish for their dramas and issues to be resolved because they feel they will be losing something by doing so.

In one sense, yes, they would be, but it's not what they think it is. They would lose a source of energy, but it's negative energy, and it does not do them any good.

The empath is not only capable of receiving feelings and energies, but also sending them. The same principal applies to people that can be used on dark entities. Send them love, joy, and warmth, and you will generally see a change in their own energies, usually for the better.

It is actually possible to affect not just individuals, but groups of people and even areas. This is one of the benefits of being empathic. You can help empower and heal negative energies.

This is something I feel should be highlighted, as most people see much information on the negative side of being an empath and very little on the benefits.

There is much benefit that being an empath can bring. It's just that we live in a world where such things are not recognized or acknowledged, making it hard for people to understand, let alone accept.

Summary

- Boundaries are limits you set for yourself that you do not allow others to go past.
- People love to push others' boundaries, but you may not be doing yourself or the other a favour by indulging them.
- An empath can not only receive feelings, but send them as well, and affect others in a positive or negative way.

Clinical Depression

The next sign of being an empath is clinical depression. It's the type of depression that no matter how strong your will power is, you just can't "get over it", and every day is a new struggle. Having suffered from such depression for around twenty or so years, I know how hard it is. Back then, no one understood that this wasn't a normal state of affairs, and I was left feeling that this was my burden to deal with.

Clinical depression certainly isn't exclusive to empaths, but you will find that there are many empaths that suffer from it. There are several reasons for such depression, and taking anti-depressants can do more harm than good, as they tend to block the empathy, but not in a good way.

As you know, the depression you suffered from was an accumulation of shock and trauma that was built up over many, many years. If we return to the analogy of a sponge collecting toxic fluids, you will have a clear picture of what an empath's energy can be like.

The reason you can't just get over it is the same as why you just can't clean a spill with the sponge. It has not been purged of all the negative substances that are within it.

The reason why empaths are much more susceptible to depression is because they tend to take things on a more personal level, and not only that, they try to not let things affect them, so they tend to push things that they should deal with away and ignore them.

Out of sight, though, is not quite out of mind. Until events that are traumatic are dealt with, the depression tends to remain, even many years later.

It can take many years of therapy, counselling, and work on the self to heal. Some practitioners might become very rich from you, especially if they don't know what they are doing.

Fortunately for the empath, Bach Flower Remedies were developed and have been nature's greatest blessing to them.

As you discovered, the Bach Flower Remedy, Star of Bethlehem can actually clear depression caused by trauma as it works to clear shock and trauma, no matter how old it is.

DEPRESSION

As there will be a section dedicated to the Bach Flower Remedies, we won't go into it too much now, except to say that many cases can be helped by this particular remedy.

So yes, being an empath will tend to make you much more vulnerable to depression.

Summary

- Empaths tend to be prone to clinical depression or depression in general.
- It may not be possible to overcome with just will power.
- The causes should be looked at and dealt with.
- Shock and trauma over a long time may lead to clinical depression.
- Empaths tend to make things worse by ignoring events as they happen, and this creates an accumulation of trauma.
- Bach Flower Remedy Star of Bethlehem clears shock and trauma.

Guilt

Another sign of being an empath is guilt. It seems that many empaths carry guilt for others, even if they have nothing to feel guilty about.

> *As you've often stated, guilt is the great destroyer, and it can bring lives to a standstill, make people fall into depression, and even make them suicidal. The empath experiences guilt on a more intense level because their natural state is to want others to be happy, and when something goes wrong, they feel they should have somehow foreseen this and prevented it.*
>
> *They also feel that if someone has taken their advice, or done something for them, which didn't work out the way they expected, then it's their fault. As a self-defence mechanism, many empaths tend to be incredible cynics.*
>
> *However, being cynical actually tends to manifest the situations that make them cynical, thus bringing about self-fulfilling prophecies. They say: I wouldn't be so cynical if I wasn't right all the time. But the reason they are right is because they are creating the circumstances for them to be right.*

> *A wonderful example of an empath is Holden Caulfield, the main character of J.D Salinger's 1951 novel, The Catcher in the Rye.*

I haven't read that book in thirty years, but I do remember him being cynical and hating everything.

> *If you read the book again, you would see a traumatized empath, affected by the death of his little brother and unable to cope in a world that seems insane to him. His depression and breakdown is a direct result of being unable to deal with his feelings and emotions, which pretty much describes many empaths.*

It pretty much describes most people, though.

> *To some degree, yes, but empaths are much more vulnerable. The higher level the empath, the more likely they are to suffer from depression and take on guilt.*

Still, he was a fictional character. I'm not sure using him as an example is really all that productive.

> *If it illustrates a point, then it works. Many points are driven home through allegories.*

So back to guilt. If I have learned one thing, it's that we carry so much guilt that it does turn us into emotional basket cases. I also learned that you can't control what other people do or how they react. All you can do is make sure that whatever you do, it's with your highest intention, and how others react is not within your control.

> *No, it's not. In fact, you are giving them experiences which help them shape themselves and gives them the opportunity to grow. Rather than feeling guilt, know that you have played a role in the long-term growth of another being. In the long run, they will thank you for it.*

From a Bach Flower perspective, the remedy Pine is amazing for clearing guilt.

Summary

- Empaths suffer quite a lot from guilt.
- They take on guilt that they are not responsible for.
- Guilt can bring lives to a standstill and lead to depression or even suicide.
- You cannot control how others react. Only how you react. As long as what you have done is with the best intention, then the rest is up to the other parties.
- Pine is the remedy for clearing guilt.

The Levels of Empathy

So, what are the levels of the empath? I call them high level empaths, but are there actually levels?

> *Levels are not so much hierarchical in nature, but more a matter of what stage of awareness and attunement the person is at. The more aware and the more attuned one is, the more activated their abilities are. Some people have chosen to have very little empathy, and that is for their own purposes and experiences. After all, you can't know your oneness with all until you've experienced not having oneness with all.*
>
> *By their very nature, all people are empathic to some degree. It's part of who they are. Most are not awakened, though. This is slowly changing as more and more people are awakening and seeking out the answers to what is happening with them.*
>
> *What you call a high level empath is simply someone who is very aware and in tune with their own empathy. That said, it does not mean they control it all that well, but they are still very empathic.*
>
> *With empathy, you will also tend to awaken other abilities such as telepathy, psychometry, clairvoyance, seeing timelines, and the other multitude of psychic abilities that exist.*

How well people are able to do those things also depends on their level of awareness and attunement, and generally, practice makes perfect. They develop a knack over time, where they can turn their abilities on and off as needed.

I've got a friend who keeps on asking me for the lottery numbers.

While he may be just joking, it is a misconception that psychics can foretell the future as nothing is set in stone. You can certainly predict probable outcomes based on picking up the information that is around now, or tuning into probable timelines, but even then, such outcomes depend on free will and choices.

As for the numbers, the nature of the lottery is meant to be random, and by asking for the numbers, they are either asking you to read the timelines, which are yet to be written, or shift them to a timeline where those numbers actually do come up.

And while it's possible to actually correctly predict those numbers, as all things are happening now, you're still working with an energy, which is intended to be completely random.

In actual fact, if you're going to win the lottery, you will win it. People don't generally win because it will change the course of their life and their goals. While money can certainly come in handy, it often blocks paths and experiences too, as people would end up bypassing experiences that they would otherwise choose to do, and thus are poorer for it.

If you are hoping and relying on gambling for that elusive win, then don't. There are plenty of other ways to generate income, which will give you both experience and satisfaction.

Summary

- Some empaths can be termed as high level. This refers to their level of awareness and attunement more than any position.
- Being an empath does not mean you can see the future, though many psychics are empathic.

Oversensitivity

The next sign of being an empath is that you feel oversensitive to whether people want you around them or not. I know I suffer from this, and I never stay where I feel I'm not needed.

> *You are actually much too sensitive in regard to this. Such things stem from your childhood years and how people treated you then. If you weren't good at sports, for instance, or felt you weren't good looking enough, or part of the in-group, then this tends to carry through.*
>
> *You did not have the best friends while growing up, as they acted as though they were ashamed to be around you, so you learned to never stay very long in one group lest they grow weary of your presence.*
>
> *Empaths can have a challenging time in regards to this. A high level empath will easily pick up any negative energies and thoughts directed towards them, and often will put the blame on themselves, and carry the guilt for that, too. They will feel that it's a failing on their part, and they should have done, or not have done something in order to make the others like them.*
>
> *This is a twisted type of logic, that not only is very unhealthy, but leads to depression, often cumulating in a meltdown. The empath goes*

into a cycle of self-loathing, believing they are not worthy of being around others, and that they don't have the right to inflict their presence on others.

Truthfully, the best thing an empath, or anyone for that matter, can do is to stop trying to fit in and please others and just state: this is who I am, and I am not going to change for you.

And yes, people will leave and fall away, and those are the people you don't want in your life in any case. But the upside is that people who do accept you will begin to come into your life and desire your presence around them.

You should never have to apologize for who you are. The empath all too often does this.

Summary

- An empath may be very sensitive to how others feel. If they feel others don't want them around, they will remove themselves.
- They will often assume that any negative energy is because it's something they have done and will blame themselves for it.
- This can lead to depression.

- It is important for the empath not to compromise themselves by trying to fit in by and not change for others.

Being Ungrounded

The next sign is that the empath feels ungrounded. If they are bored, or they really don't want to be somewhere, they will often escape by retreating to their imagination and travel to distant and far off places, often in other worlds or galaxies. Anywhere but here, basically.

> *I'd argue that this is not just an empath trait. Plenty of non-empaths have done similarly when they are bored. The main difference here is where they go in their minds. The low level empath might well focus on worldly stuff, such as sports, their partners (potential or otherwise), or their hobbies. The high level empath has more of a tendency to travel away from this world and life.*
>
> *This is a form of astral travelling with the mind. Some call it mind travelling, some call it mind-scaping. It's part of your essence travelling to another place, time, or dimension and interacting there, or just observing.*
>
> *It's quite common with psychics, though many dismiss it as daydreaming, but as you well know, it's real and can affect things on both the astral and the physical level.*

I've found that the stronger the pull to something, the more real it appears to be.

Generally, yes, though it's all real. Many answers about your past and why you are here in this life can be found out by following the stories you experience while mind travelling.

But aren't they just stories that we make up as we go along?

You're making it all up as you go along. What do you think the process of creation is? Just because you're doing it on another level doesn't mean that it's not valid. Just because people believe that this third dimension level is the only reality, it doesn't mean it is so. We should be glad it is not so, for if this was all that is, then there would be very little point to it.

Okay, so is mind travelling useful to an empath, and is it safe?

Define useful and define safe.

Useful, as in it helps them cope with their empathy and safe as in no harm can come of it.

Mind travelling is a tool, and how you use this tool depends on how useful it is to the empath. Where your focus is, is generally where you are, though we are multi-dimensional beings that exist on many levels at once. As the focus is generally on this 3D level, you will have your awareness mainly here.

> *If you decide to mind travel, or you get a pull to experience what appears to be a fantasy or daydream, it will be the nature of what you are doing that defines if it's useful for being an empath. It very much depends on what you are trying to achieve.*

That's not really an answer. Just yes or no would be enough.

> *It would be, but then you'd have to explain why. If you use mind travelling to visit others on the astral levels, and it's for the purpose of gathering information about them in order to assist them, or to help them with dealing with negative energies, then yes, it's useful. Is this an empathic ability? No, though the empath can take the information that they gather, extract the feelings they get from it, and use that to help another, or use it to make their next decision on what they should do.*

> *On that subject, when you connect to something, it's wise to only connect for as long as you need to in order to gain the information you are seeking. If you stay connected, or you forget to disconnect, you may have the energies affecting your own, or draining you on an energetic level.*

> *Thus, it is important to disconnect from any energy source you are investigating, unless it's*

> *a source that helps uplift and renew your own energies, such as nature or your higher energies.*
>
> *This also helps answer the second questions as to whether it is safe. While you can't really harm your soul as it goes, you can affect it in ways that are undesirable. The feelings of being drained, or being bombarded by negative energies is not one that can cheerfully be sustained for long periods without it having detrimental effects on your emotional wellbeing, not to mention the physical.*

This brings to mind an incident that occurred back in 2004, where one of my online friends said she was feeling back pain and was drained. I had just recently understood that my mind travels were real, so I offered to take a look at her. She accepted, and I got the impression of a black giant spider on her back. I asked her to look at what she saw there (as she is psychic, too) and she saw the same thing. I offered to help remove it from her, and she accepted. Though I did not tell her what I was doing, she said she felt something lift the moment I managed to shift it. When I looked into this a bit more, as to why this had happened, I found out from another source that you can pick up such things by mind travelling through space. I questioned her about this, and she told me that when she was bored with her factory job, she would often go flying through space in her mind.

I guess that would be an example of where you need to be careful.

Yes, it is, and it's a good example. Many of these types of entities do get into your energy fields and feed off of you there. You certainly have your fair share of them, though you seem oblivious to them unless you take the trouble to look. Removing them is a matter of simply sending love and light to the entity and commanding that it remove itself. You just need to state that you no longer agree to be fed upon. It may not do so without your permission. But you must be absolute about it. You cannot allow doubt, fear, or compassion for its needs (such as you believe they are) to undermine your decision.

One thing to point out, though, is that some people have put seals in place that look like spiders, or are black in nature. The seals are in energetic spots in our energy centres, and if we choose to remove them before we are ready, we may well unleash more energy than we are ready to take on, which can lead to burn out, and by burn out, I mean burn out on an emotional, psychic, or even a body level.

So if you see something black, do not automatically assume it's an attack. You will feel if you should leave it in place. The seals will be removed when the right time comes.

So, no, mind travel is not always safe, but it's safer than an out of body experience, where you can be very much subjected to the realities of a stronger presence. This can still happen while mind travelling, too, but your body helps ground you, and it's much harder to become trapped, or drawn into something you did not intend.

In any case, if you proceed with love and pure intent, and do not allow fear to rule you, you will always come out of it fine.

So, there's a chance that you might not come out of fine?

Ultimately, all will be fine. It's not possible for it not to end up with everyone not returning to who they really are. There are things along the way, though, that can make the journey much more complex and traumatic than need be. The greatest danger is that people can become trapped in a reality that might be akin to their concept of Hell. Hell being the complete absence of God in your life, or rather, the perceived lack of absence, as no one is ever abandoned. It's not even possible for that to happen.

If you play with things you do not understand fully, you can inadvertently create responses that are not pleasant.

Like eating an unbalanced diet or a diet of junk food? You end up feeling lousy and your body hates you for it?

> *As a simplistic analogy, then yes. Still, the rules for dealing with psychic abilities and astral levels are simple:*
>
> *Always remember your oneness with all that is.*
>
> *Always come from a place of love from within.*
>
> *Never try to force your own reality on others.*
>
> *Never judge that you see. What is is, and it is for a reason.*
>
> *Never be attached to the end results. Hold the intention in mind, and enjoy the journey.*
>
> *You would be amazed how many people do not follow those rules. Always be gentle and remember that all you see if simply another part of who you are.*

And if we don't do this, is it a bad thing?

> *There is no 'bad'. There is simply what you create and the consequences. If something is what you did not wish to experience, then you might consider it 'bad'. If it's something that you did, then you might consider it 'good'. Still, good and bad are strictly relative, and what*

one might term as bad may turn out to be a blessing, and vice versa.

I'm just saying that if you wish to be in harmony with the results of your actions, then this is a good way to do it. You don't have to do it that way. You can simply choose to ignore this advice, and you will still come out of it just fine, it just might take a lot longer than you would have wished it to.

So, any last words for the empath on this subject?

Just the standard advice. Whatever you decide to do, let it be a reflection of who you really are. Be it. Don't do it. When you are being it, nothing can stop you.

Still, the last words should be on the subject of being ungrounded, which is what this section is about.

The empath is generally ungrounded due to not wishing to be here, and that generally is due to a lack of self-confidence, though, as pointed out, boredom is also a factor.

The lack of self-confidence is actually one of the major factors so many empaths face. It's a strange fact that people do not accept their own experiences as being real. They would rather listen to someone else, who will tell them that it is all in their imagination, rather than believe in their own evidence.

Are you suggesting that they should believe everything they experience? I know that from my own experiences, things certainly aren't always what they appear to be.

No, I'm saying to not let other people decide what is true for them. Truth is very individual, and there are exceptions to rules for everything. This is because people not only live in a co-created reality, but they also live in their own individually made reality. Just because you don't agree with it doesn't mean that it's not so for them.

There are people who just love to invalidate others, just because they can. These people can be very harmful to others, especially sensitive people.

Now, it's fair to say that there are many wonders in this world, and it's also fair to say that some of them certainly aren't what they appear to be, especially where the astral levels are concerned. So it's very important to trust in what you are feeling, and also be aware that feelings on a subject may change, depending on what new information appears, or if something about the situation changes.

If someone tells you something, and it feels right to you, then it's right for you. However, there are many times when we accept another's word, just because we somehow feel they know better than us, even if we are not feeling the truth of the matter. When we don't feel the truth of the matter, we tend to ignore it and some even become fanatic about it, as though more people believing in their truths will make it true.

But truth has no need to be believed by the general populous. It just is, and it will always be regardless of what others say about it.

One of the greatest truths is that we are all creators, and we create all the time with everyone in every moment. So what we have constructed may not be what another has constructed, but none the less, both realities are perfectly valid. Why should one be preferred over another, just because someone doesn't agree with you?

As empaths, you are able to not only create on a more intense level, and by that I mean, what you are creating can manifest much faster, but you are also able to perceive so much more than one who has not attuned to those abilities.

A colour-blind person will see colours differently than one who is not colour blind. Are both wrong? Is one right and the other is wrong? Or are both right? The answer is that they are experiencing the evidence of their own reality for whatever soul agenda they have. Both are perfectly valid, and truth be told, even the one who is not colour blind does not see all the colours and vibrancy that is really out there. So is their version of reality any truer?

So I say to you, the empath who is reading this, trust in what you sense. Trust in what you feel. You are experiencing this for a reason, and you know that your reality is real to you, and that is enough.

One of the things I've always liked is the question: Who can make me a better offer?

Yes. If you're happy with your reality and it's working for you, why would you want to give it up for something that may be empty and shallow for you?

Now, the thing with being confident is that you should be quietly confident. It's probably unproductive to suddenly start going about proclaiming that you are an empath and you can do things others can't. Doing this will create annoyance, resentment and a sense of separation and elitism.

On the other hand, you should not have to hide it either. If it comes up, just be matter of fact about it. Don't turn it into a big deal. Just let others know this is what you experience, and you are not the only one. In fact, you might help awaken others to their own experience, or even help them to understand that they have been having the same things occur, but they always dismissed it as fantasy.

The key is to help others remember and awaken. We are now in a period of our history where it's okay to be this way. The world is starting to awaken. True, there are still many who will insist that you are mad, in league with Satan, possessed by an evil spirit, or simply deluded, but a time is coming where such abilities will become the norm, and they will be accepted as a birth right.

I know many people who say that such powers are a gift from God, and if they are abused, they can be taken away.

Depends on what you believe. In actual fact, all is God. God does not choose who to give powers to and who to take it away from. You choose for yourself. And you choose by how you choose to use your powers.

If powers are abused, then yes, there are consequences, but that is universal law, and not God punishing you for it.

Psychics in general, do not so much lose their powers, but become unattuned to them. If they start to fake things, make them up, or their ego starts to make them believe that they are somehow better than the rest, and creates the illusion of separation, then yes, they may well start to experience a loss of power.

What is really happening, though, is that they are no longer in tune with the energies. They are no longer in harmony with what is really going on.

Many suggest that charging for psychic services will make you lose your powers, but it is not the charging of money that makes this happen. What often happens is that when the psychic can't deliver for some reason, they then make it up. What should happen is that they say, I'm sorry, it's just not happening today, and refund the money.

Another reason is that ego takes over and they forget to listen to both client and the spirit, and end up thinking they know the answers, even if they are completely wrong.

In any case, we are off topic now as we should be discussing grounding.

Other causes for being ungrounded can be: shock, exhaustion, fear, guilt, and anything that makes you not want to be 'here'. It is the desire not to be here which creates being ungrounded in the first place.

There are some other ways to ground yourself. One is to find an activity you enjoy. The key here is that it should be something physical. This could be exercising, sports, interacting with people whose company you enjoy, or doing an activity that just allows you be here.

And of course, Bach Flower Remedies.

Which we will look at in another section of this book.

Summary

- An empath may become ungrounded if they do not wish to be here.
- This can be due to shock, trauma, fears, etc.
- Self-confidence is one of the main keys to grounding.

Picking up on Other People's Feelings

This is one of the primary traits of an empath. They will often pick up on the feelings of others around them, though they may not realize it.

Those who do, though, can always tell how someone is feeling, even if they tell you a different story. It's very hard to fool an empath in this manner.

> *This goes back to empaths picking up on each other and loved ones. Once you define your boundaries, it becomes much easier to know how someone is doing by just focusing on them. Once again, practice helps a lot. The more you do it, the more you can do it, but remember, it's very easy to get lost in another's energies.*
>
> *The best technique, if you wish to check on someone, is to connect to them for a moment, and then examine the information. You don't need to put your hand into a flame for more than an instance to know that it's hot, and keeping your hand there will definitely damage you.*
>
> *Sometimes it may take time to consolidate the information, and things may not be clear for maybe a day or more, but once it is done, you will be pretty certain what the truth of a matter certainly is.*

This technique can be very useful for knowing if people are telling you the truth, trying to manipulate you, or just trying to feed you their own false stories.

Summary

- An empath can pick up on how other people feel.
- It is a good practice to only connect momentarily if you wish to check on someone.
- This can also be useful for seeing if someone is being truthful or not.

Giving Others the Benefit of the Doubt

That brings me to the next sign, which is that the empath tends to give people the benefit of the doubt. You give them every chance to prove themselves before doing what must be done, just in case you're wrong about them or have judged them unfairly.

> *This is actually a sense of guilt, a fear of being wrong and a fear of hurting someone by your actions that allows this to happen.*
>
> *Many people can argue convincingly and turn black into white, and they always have a perfectly valid reason for doing, or not doing something.*
>
> *The empath wants to give them the benefit of the doubt because they feel they don't have all the information.*
>
> *For example, what if the person is having a hard time at home? What if they aren't feeling well? What if they genuinely have tried, but haven't quite got it yet.*
>
> *What we are doing is taking responsibility away from the other party and putting it all upon ourselves. We are saying: It's not their fault. It's never their fault, and it is us who should adjust rather than them who should honour their agreements.*

The fact is, most non-empathic people would happily take you down the moment they feel they are not getting what they want out of things.

You will feel the truth of what is going on. You have to trust in it. If someone is out to cheat you, or abuse your trust or generosity, then you are not doing them any favours by indulging them and you're certainly not doing yourself any favours either. You will just end up angry and resentful because of it.

This world, right now, tends to take advantage of what they consider weakness and of those who will freely give of themselves.

I know that I'd rather people do the right thing by me, because it is the right thing to do, and not because they are forced to do so.

You are assuming that they consider the right thing to do is what you consider the right thing is. Most people rarely think with that in mind. They see their own advantage in mind first, and if that conflicts with doing what is in your interest, then they will tend to choose their own interests ahead of yours.

The irony of this type of thinking is that they actually do hurt themselves by doing so, because not only do they lose out in the long term, but they also create the illusion of separation and the belief that there is not enough to go around, when in fact there is.

You can't make someone act in a certain way if they do not wish to. History has shown that over and over again. All you can do is work to change their core belief system, and bring a different perspective to them.

Now, that being said, the responsibility is also on you to not be taken advantage of. You know when something isn't right for you, and you also know when someone is playing you for a gullible fool.

It is up to you to say enough is enough. You can be diplomatic about how you do this, but do yourself a favour and say 'no more'. Let them prove to you that they will honour their agreements, and not the other way around.

I think that one of the reasons we don't do that, or confront the person, is because we fear we will lose something because of it. We may not be getting a lot, but we may lose what we already have if we make waves. Certainly in this day and age, you can easily be replaced by another in a heartbeat.

You're assuming that you can't progress, or that you don't have the abilities to thrive. Fact is, not only do you have those abilities, but it's your right to do so. You need to bear in mind that nothing is random. You are not in a place that is not of your making. If you believe that you are not capable, and that others must be there for you to survive, then you are creating a reality where this is so.

Sometimes, though, you will be forced to move on and let people go. Not because you want to, but because you can't progress if you don't. No change is ever for the worst, in spite of what it might seem to be at the time. Life is a progression, and our soul aspect always seeks to grow and evolve. It can't do that if it's stuck in one place.

The question you must ask yourself is this: Is this the kind of life I wish to live?

If the answer is 'no' then set the intention for change and follow the synchronicities that occur.

If the answer is 'yes' then continue on with what you are doing, but don't complain. Remember, you have created this, and are continuing to choose it.

Summary

- An empath has a tendency to always give others the benefit of the doubt.
- People tend to abuse this and use the empath.

- We should take responsibility for when to say ‘no’ to someone.
- An empath may be reluctant to say ‘no’ because they fear confrontation and loss.

Strong Connection to Nature and Animals

The next sign is that you feel a great connection to animals and nature. You may even sense the energy of an area.

> *It's true that empaths will feel a greater connection to such things, though it's foolish to say that only empaths could do so. There are people who love nature and animals for its own sake.*
>
> *What an empath will find, though, is that they are able to connect to the energies of such things. When an empath connects to non-human things, be it an animal, insect, arachnid, plant, mineral, or even vegetable, they are able to pick up on the energies that it sends out.*
>
> *As everything is alive with the energy of life, and it's all the same stuff that makes up all of it, the empath can resonate on those energetic levels.*
>
> *There are distinct advantages and disadvantages, too, to being able to do this.*
>
> *Plants can thrive and provide energy and healing, not to mention knowledge and wisdom when you connect to their source.*
>
> *Rocks, crystals and stones all have their own particular vibrational qualities that can either*

help, or hinder you, depending on what your goal is. Treat them with love and respect, and you will feel which one is good for you.

Animals will very much depend on what they are, and what they sense from you. There is no such thing as 'dumb' animals. They may not always have the level of awareness that some other creatures may possess, but they all have own unique connection and purpose.

I had an interesting experience the other week. I was starting to hear knocking noises coming from the roof during the night. The last time I heard something like that, it turned out there were rats living in the roof, and they can sound like they are going to break through the ceiling with the noise they make.

I pondered what I should do, and decided to try sending a message for them to move out, as I didn't want to hurt them. I haven't heard anything since then.

The message was received and accepted. They did indeed move away. This is not your only experience with such things occurring. You've also done similar things with spiders and a bee. You have asked the spiders to leave the space they were in, stating that you did not wish to harm them, and they were gone the very next time you entered the room.

> *The bee was in your car, and seeking a way out, but could not find its way past the back window. You sent it a visual message showing it the way out, and it immediately took it.*
>
> *There is little to fear when you are in tune with nature, and the more connected you are, the greater your communication and oneness becomes.*

Ironically, I've had a hard time connecting with nature as a rule. Empath or not, I can't always seem to feel or sense it.

> *There are different levels of attunement. You are certainly highly attuned to the Bach Flower Remedies, and you can be sure that's nature in its purest essence.*
>
> *Land, which includes houses, rooms, or any large space, such as a suburb, city, country, is particularly interesting for the empath. Someone who is attuned can literally feel the energies change as they move from place to place. They don't even need to be in the area. All they need to do is shift their focus to the spot, and they will get a snapshot of the energy there.*
>
> *This has many uses. For example if you are house hunting, you can detect if a place will be right for you. If you walk in, and you feel uneasy, or your skin starts to prickle and crawl,*

then get out as soon as you can. There is something bad with the energy, and it will not benefit you to stay.

It is possible, if you're a strong enough sender, to cleanse the area of that energy, though unless you are called to do so, you're best to leave well enough alone.

It's also useful when you sense there is tension in a room. You can often shift or transmute it with your own positive energies.

As mentioned, you can also pick up on if the energy of an area is good or not. You can also pick up spots of high-level energy where the source is renewing.

The empath is served by finding a place where the energy feels good to them. It also helps protect them against negative influences.

I know you say you can change the energy if it's bad, especially when you can "cut the air with a knife." But how exactly do you do that? I know I can do it, but I couldn't explain to someone how it's done.

The key is to be the source, and then expand that energy. There are some points to consider here.

Do not try and force energy on another, or on a situation. It does not work, and all you are trying to do is force your will on another, or on a circumstance that you may know nothing about. If you try to force your will upon others, it will make the situation worse, and just leave you frustrated.

Always come from a non-judgmental perspective. In other words, do not judge if something is good or bad, just simply observe and feel. If you sense that it would be everyone's interest to transmute the energies, and then do so by being love and peace and projecting it. You can do this quietly and, indeed, you should. Be calm. Be serene. Know that all is as it should be, and that you may have been called specifically for this purpose.

Now it's worth noting that in order to use this technique, you must be able to be what you are trying to manifest, and if you have unresolved issues, or a lack of understanding on what is upsetting you, then you may fail, as those issues will tend to come up and frustrate and anger you.

Many empaths require healing, and as stated, the Bach Flower Remedies are wonderful for doing this.

One technique I've seen used is to visualize clouds being drawn away. Another is the sending of light to the area affected, and yet another is simply prayer, which is even more powerful when done by two or more people.

> *Those are good techniques, but once again, it's simply being the source. If a technique works for you, then use it. It's important to be without agenda when transmuting, otherwise you will most likely corrupt the energies with your own desires, and that can often make things worse.*

In what way?

> *By producing outcomes that were not expected or desired.*

Summary

- Empaths often feel a stronger connection to nature and animals.
- One who is in tune with nature can gain much wisdom.
- An empath can sense if an area is healthy to be around or not and guide their decisions when doing such activities as house hunting, etc.
- Empaths can clear or transmute negative energy to positive energy.
- When clearing energy, it's important to be without expectations as this can produce undesired outcomes.

Feeling the Pain and Suffering of Others

Okay, onto the next sign. When someone is in distress, pain, or is suffering, you will automatically feel bad with them, and even take on sympathy pains. You also will sympathize with them.

> *This actually goes a lot deeper than you feeling bad just because they wish to feel bad. There are empaths that will be chameleons, that is, change to match whoever they happen to be talking to.*
>
> *On the surface, these people always are in agreement with you, no matter what your point of view may be, but when left to their own devises, they often have a completely different perspective to the one they have shown.*
>
> *The Chameleon Empath, as I call them, wants to be everybody's friend. They desire everyone to be happy, and will do so in any way possible.*
>
> *It can be very frustrating dealing with someone like that, as you never really get anywhere with them and you can never really trust what they tell you.*

Well, no, I suppose not. But I think we're a bit off the subject of this sign here.

No, not really. It's the flipside of the same coin. The reason the Chameleon Empath is like that is because they hate to see others suffer. They feel that sympathizing and even taking on the pain of others, at least while in their presence, will somehow make them feel better and for a short while they do, at least until they leave the room and find out later that the opposing view has just been taken by the same person they confided in.

In Bach Flower terms, this type of person would be a Centaury type, that is, unable to say 'no' with a touch of Pine (guilt) thrown in.

Sympathy pains can also be borne out of fear. You feel the pain because somewhere you also fear that you may have the same condition, or will eventually develop it. Of course, this is not true for all cases. For instance, a man having sympathy pain for his pregnant partner obviously does not fear being pregnant. The energies of the partners though, are very strongly connected.

Still, too many empaths live their lives in perpetual fear, and sympathy pains may be a symptom of that fear.

Could they also be used as a warning that something is wrong with your body?

> *Yes, they can be. If you resonate with something, it's normally because you are matched on a vibrational level, that is, your energies are similar. Still, don't start panicking just because you happen to feel such pains. They do not automatically mean you have their condition.*

Okay, so what do we do about them? I'm pretty sure they are beyond the control of most empaths.

> *One solution is a matter of the flow of energy in your body. It may indicate a blockage, and such blockages can lead to dis-ease.*

I recall, back in the early 1990s, a friend and I went to a 2 day workshop on energy, which was conducted by a Taoist. I wouldn't have called him a master as such, though. One thing he did do was take us through an energy meditation, where we were moving energies throughout our body.

As I got to the heart area, I started to feel a strong sense of panic and extreme discomfort on an energy level, like there was something I did not want to face. I had a very strong urge to stand up and rush outside, however I'm a stubborn person, and I didn't allow that as a viable option.

All of a sudden, I felt something shift, as though a drain had been unblocked and all the energies suddenly flowed through it.

I remembered that the feeling I had just had was exactly the same as when I looked at diabetes. I had an irrational fear of it back then, and could not even face the possibility of testing it.

When I checked those feelings again, I found that was clear, too.

I came to the conclusion that the two were connected, and it was possible that dis-ease was caused by a blockage in the flow of energy, which, if I think about it, is what many say, and what you just said yourself.

> *There are many blockages, which stem from our lifestyles. We do not know how to look after our bodies, and we ignore them when they are asking for what they need, taking pleasure over health.*
>
> *Back to the main point, if the empath does feel sympathy pains, they should try to look and see if there is an energy blockage there. It may be difficult to face, but if it isn't faced, it can have long-term consequences, much like emotional pain and trauma.*

Okay, how do you clear such blockages?

> *There are a few methods. Acupuncture is traditionally used for getting the energies flowing through the body's meridians again. You can meditate, as you did, and visualize the energies flowing along the pathways, though*

that needs a degree of guidance or mastery to do successfully. Some exercises such as Tai Chi, which focuses on energy movement can be very beneficial, but in the end, your lifestyle and diet are always key to your health. Fear, worry, anger, stress, especially stress, will slowly deplete the body of its vital nutrients and hurt it in the long run.

What about those people who actually take on the conditions of those around them. How does that work?

There are a few reasons for this occurring.

So, they actually do take on the illness on a physical level?

Yes, it does happen. Once again, it depends on the person. For instance, if you recall, your father had a very bad back, and your mother always wished she could take the pain away from him by taking it on herself. When his spirit moved on, it wasn't too long after that she did indeed develop chronic back issues, which have stayed with her to this day.

She gave her body permission to have issues, partly out of love, partly out of guilt that she couldn't help him in any other way.

Another reason is that sensitive people can adjust their own vibrational resonance with the person they are linking with, and that leaves them open to the same type of conditions and illnesses.

This is often done out of compassion, but it does not actually help either party, unless the empath is skilled enough to heal themselves, and heal the other party along with them. Sometimes there may be what you call divine intervention, and one or all are healed.

This is not as uncommon as you may believe.

The main cause, though, is that the energies are matching. Everything is simply vibration, and the way things vibrate determines what the object or matter actually is.

This is transmutation. Changing one energy into another. We do it all the time on some levels, especially with our body, though it is generally over many years.

Summary

- Empaths often feel the pain and suffering of others.
- Some empaths are like chameleons and change according to the people around them.
- Empaths generally hate to see others suffer.

- Some empaths may feel sympathy pains.
- Sympathy pains can also be a warning that there is an energy blockage within the empath's body.
- An empath can also match their energies with another and take on their condition. An empath who is skilled in healing can heal others by healing themselves.

Desire to Help Others

The next sign is you may have an overwhelming desire to help and save others from themselves.

> *That occurs with many types of people. Empaths certainly do fall into that category. A high level empath can go several ways. They can be self-destructive, that is, they try to hurt themselves by hurting others, they can be balanced and understand that all is as it should be, or they can want to save the world because they cannot abide pain and suffering, and they wish for all to be happy.*
>
> *Actually, people, and especially the media, tend to use the word 'suffering' very loosely. Suffering is often a matter of perspective and while someone may be in pain, or unpleasant circumstances, it does not automatically mean they are suffering. Things are often sensationalized because people love their dramas.*
>
> *On those empaths who wish to help others, there tend to be two types: One who helps from a genuine perspective and without condition and the other who does it out of ego, to curry favour and make others indebted to them.*
>
> *The latter should be avoided if at all possible. They are not really interested in making things better for you; they are more about making*

things more comfortable for themselves. They will judge your circumstances based on their own belief systems, and decide that what you really need is what they really need, though they will not admit that to themselves.

As nothing is random, (unless the intention is to make it as such, which in itself is randomness within order), those who find themselves in horrible circumstances have entered it of their own volition, though normally they are not aware of this.

Nothing occurs to us that is not fully known or comprehended on our higher soul level. Those levels are so fine, though, that they are very difficult to tap into and bring down to this 3D energy level.

Now, this may seem like a harsh thing to hear for many people, as they will protest saying: well, I didn't ask for this accident, or I did not ask for my loved ones to die, and what have you. And for many cases, this will seemingly be so.

The thing is, though, that with free will, and the freedom to create whatever we wish, we cannot find ourselves in circumstances that were not of our making. For that to occur, free will could not exist, as that would not be your choice.

To every event in one's life, there is gift, and an experience that will help them be who they desire to be and though they may not see it at the time, they will see it later on, even if that is during their life review when they have left their current body.

That being said, the empath who charges in and tries to fix another, especially without being asked to, is doing no one a service. (They are, however, having the experience of when to act or when not to act, though many will take lifetimes to understand this.)

When someone is in difficult circumstances, they are experiencing what they have created. Most of the time it is what they need, and what is needed in order for them to gain the critical experience to do and be what they desire to be. But there are many times when things get out of control, and they no longer wish to be in such circumstances. That is when they ask for help. That is when they ask for healing. That is when they send out a soul call.

Soul calls have been covered elsewhere, but to recap, it's a call for help on a soul level and is often answered by another, who will come into the sender's life, and help them past the current difficulties.

As an empath, when you wish to help someone, you should always consider if there is a calling to help. Is there an irresistible pull to help? Is it difficult or impossible to ignore it? Such things are soul calls, and can often be confused with falling in love, though once the soul call is over, the feeling of love also tends to fade.

Yes, I've had lots of soul calls in my life. It's much easier when you know what is going on.

I can't help but notice that you seem to be quite hard on empaths. This is meant to be a document to help them.

They are observations. It is neither good nor bad. It just is. There is little point in sugar coating things. You are not doing anyone any services by doing so. What this book is about is pointing out the pitfalls of being an empath, and what can be done to avoid them. Many people find empathy very difficult to cope with, and these are some of the reasons why.

When it's used in a positive manner, your life can flourish, but if the person becomes bogged down with the drama and feels like a victim, then it can be a terrible curse.

Summary

- Empaths often have an overwhelming desire to help others.

- Unless one is called to do so, the empath should not try and 'fix' someone without their permission.
- Empaths often receive soul calls, which is a call for help from one soul to another.

Ability to Sense Lies and Deception

The next sign is the ability to tell when someone is lying, or doing something behind your back. Personally, I've found this pretty useful over the years, as when the crap hit the fan, I was not taken by surprise.

> *An empath can often feel when something is true or not. They can sense when a person is playing them for a fool or is genuine. It is worth noting at the outset, though, that sometimes it can take a while for the empath to decipher the information and work out what it all means. The more experienced you are with it, the quicker you can do this.*
>
> *While it's true that most people can detect something that isn't true, empaths tend to pick up more information because they can feel the other's intentions. It's not always going to be clear what is going on, though. Sometimes you will have an uneasy feeling that something isn't right.*

I used to get that when I left work a lot some years ago. I'd feel very anxious about things, in spite of the fact my work was good and I was doing way more than my fair share. I would find out afterwards, thanks to friends and other methods that there were a few people who were assassinating my character behind my back. It was never pleasant, and when things came to a head, I was always the bad guy, it would seem.

> *It is fair to say that those attacks on you were unwarranted, and as you did not retaliate, the attackers were dealt with as per their own karmic outcomes. None of them are there today. The point is, though, it never took you by surprise.*

The hard part was trying to work out why I was getting those feelings, and who was involved, though, I did get helpful messages from my guides from time to time telling me who was doing what, which later proved to be correct.

> *When things are being done behind your back, it does take some doing to find out exactly what is going on. You may feel that something isn't right, and you will sense that something unpleasant is occurring, but you may not understand the nature of it.*
>
> *One method you can use is the 20 questions type method. You have a list of questions that you ask yourself, and see which ones feel right. Of course, you don't limit yourself to twenty questions, but you do use the same technique to get answers.*
>
> *When you hit on the right path, you will feel a sense of truth and often a lessening of the anxiety that you feel. When you hit the right*

answer, you will feel something 'click' within your mind and your feelings. You may not have any rational reason to believe the answer, but it should be certainly taken seriously.

It is also very important that you don't have an attachment to what the answer is. If you wish for a certain outcome, you will possibly bias the results, and you will end up with an answer that will not aid you.

The other thing about getting to the truth is that it doesn't always happen right away. Someone may well convince you that something is so, and you will accept it at the time, but when you walk away, you will start to feel as though something wasn't right.

Two things are occurring here. One, you are no longer being influenced by their energy and focus, and as an empath, you will be highly susceptible to someone forcing their energies upon you. This occurs quite frequently, and is often a technique salespeople use in order to push sales through at the time. Get the sale there and then and stop the potential buyer from walking away and really giving it some thought.

The other thing is you being attuned to what is going on. This is the process of your energies coming into synchronization with the other party's energies, and seeing how it relates to you.

Then, suddenly, you will just know what is true or if someone is being deceitful, pretending to be something they are not, or telling you what you want to hear. There is often a window of opportunity the deceiver will have to convince you to do something for them, and during that time, be it minutes, hours, days, weeks, months, or even years, you are vulnerable.

However, once that window closes, it is extremely hard to ever fool you again. You will always be aware when they try.

Why can it sometimes take years? Because sometimes the person truly, really, believes what they are saying to you. They may be completely wrong and they may not have a clue what they are talking about, but you will accept it because you pick up that they believe it.

Hence, it is always important to check your own truth, your own feelings, and your intuition.

One final and very important note here is to remember that feelings change. They can change on a moment-to-moment basis. What might feel right to you now, may suddenly feel wrong to you tomorrow. And what might feel wrong to you now, might suddenly feel right to you tomorrow.

This does not mean you were wrong, it means you have picked up on new data, or it may mean that something has changed or entered into the equation that you are not aware of. It means that you have attuned. It means that you are now in synch with the information that you need to be aware of.

It's very hard to fool an empath for long, especially one who knows how to listen to their feelings and sense the truth behind things.

Summary

- Empaths have a built-in lie detector.
- They can often sense when something is going on behind their backs.
- They may feel anxiety for no apparent reason.
- Using the 'twenty questions' technique, they can generally work out where the source is coming from.
- It is important not to be attached to any outcomes.
- If a person believes what they are saying is true, then the empath will also pick that up as truth, even if it's not accurate.

- Feelings can change on a moment-to-moment basis, so what you feel is true today, may not be so tomorrow.

Ability to Heal Others

The next sign is that many empaths are natural healers. They can heal others by tuning in to what they need and sending healing energies. Sometimes they can even lay hands and help heal that way.

> *Healing energies are normally very high-level abilities. While we all have an innate ability to heal ourselves and others, we tend to not do so because we are too busy trying to take energy rather than letting it flow through us.*
>
> *Psychic healing, remote healing, healing with prayers, and healing by tapping into the energies to know what is needed really does work. It really does exist and you've certainly experienced this both ways.*
>
> *The first rule of healing is: You can't heal another; you can only enable them to heal themselves. We are not talking about temporary healing here; we are talking about permanent healing. It's easy to heal someone's pain, stop a condition from flaring up, and so forth, but unless the lifestyle and causes are dealt with, it is no more than a temporary stop gap at best.*

I've used the example of being a leaky bucket. You can fill it with water, but unless you plug up the holes, the water will drain away, and it doesn't matter how much water you pour into it, it will never fix the issues. I think many people are leaky buckets.

> *It's a good analogy. It is true that many actually resist healing, and keep themselves in a state of ill health in order to avoid facing certain things in life. There is an abundance of reasons for this, and there is no judgement on them. It's just life. For someone to heal, they have to be ready to do so.*
>
> *It is also true that many people have conditions and dis-ease because they have a specific agenda in mind. They may well be experiencing the condition in order to gain greater insight and understanding to it.*
>
> *One example that would apply to you is that you suffered from depression for a long time, but this enabled you to find a cure. If you had never been depressed, you would not have been able to do so. You also were certainly ready for this as you no longer secretly enjoyed being sad and were determined to find out how to heal it.*

Yes, that was the clinical depression, which I healed with the Bach Flower Remedy, Star of Bethlehem. I have spent a good part of my life searching for cures and answers. I could never accept that something was incurable, or that there was nothing anyone could do about it.

> *Empaths can be natural healers by virtue of being able to tap into the patient's energies and sense what they need. If they are wise, the healer will attempt to learn all that they can about medical conditions and the treatments out there. The more they know, the more attuned they become and the greater the mastery.*
>
> *They then will be able to apply that knowledge by picking up on what the other person may need.*
>
> *Also, the healer can send prayers and energies to the patient. Once again, this must never be forced and it's best to set the intention and allow the healing to take place naturally.*

I've seen that kind of thing happen a few times. Two incidences stand out in my mind. The first was back in 1997, when I was at a friend's place. He suffered from problems with his kidneys, and that night he was in a lot of pain. He had forgotten his medicine, and he was considering going to the hospital. I very casually sent him healing energies to his kidney area. There wasn't much force behind it; it was just a sending of energies.

Within a short while, my friend suddenly announced that he must have been mistaken about his kidneys, as the pain had gone, and he was feeling better. I didn't tell him what I did, but the results did surprise me.

The other one was when I was married. My 10-year old step daughter suddenly started having incredibly painful stomach cramps during the evening. We took her to the children's hospital and waited for a couple of hours to be attended to. But it must have been a busy night, or they were short staffed as no one actually attended to her. Every few minutes, she'd scream out in extreme pain.

At around 1 am, I felt the pull to focus energy on her stomach. I found myself drawing a spiral in an anti-clockwise direction. I did this for about a minute, and then suddenly, she had to go to the bathroom and move her bowels. She was perfectly fine after that. It was just a case of constipation, I think, but the fact that things came good right after I sent the healing always stuck in my mind.

> *Yes, those were good examples, and you did indeed bring relief. Though, for your friend, it was only temporary as he needed to change his lifestyle, and wouldn't. As a healer, you are quite potent, much more than you realize. It's a potential everybody has, but it is fair to say that you are very self-realized in that ability as those who have received healing from you will attest to.*

If the empath is interested in healing, they will find their empathic abilities extremely useful, regardless of what method they use.

Summary

- High-level Empaths tend to be natural healers.
- They can heal remotely. Distance is often no barrier.
- Unless the subject is ready to heal, any healing will be of a temporary nature.

Not Feeling Like You Belong

On to the next sign. You feel like you don't belong to this world. You'll often feel like a fish out of water and that you just don't fit in. There is a sense of being alone. Many feel like they are an alien.

> *This is due to the illusion of separation and varying levels of awareness. The empath can feel, see and comprehend what many others cannot. They feel alone because they are not amongst others who can understand and validate who they are.*
>
> *Sometimes this is true, sometimes it isn't, and the empath is blocked off due to fear or trauma or some other factor.*
>
> *An empath who sees themselves as part of it all will rarely feel alone or that they don't belong. They will see and understand their place in the scheme of things and know that they are not there by random chance.*
>
> *There is a danger for the empath to be seduced by victimhood: They versus an uncaring world that does not understand, while the empath struggles valiantly on against the odds.*
>
> *It's seductive and dangerous as it is a path of destruction. While the world may not understand who they are, they are also*

allowing the world to separate them by not understanding what it is.

People want to be angry. They want the dramas, the excitement, the passion, the challenges, the triumphs against all the odds, and there's nothing wrong with that. Sooner or later, they will become weary and seek another way.

So… they are not really aliens? Just humans who misunderstand their connections?

What is an alien? The very term implies separation. If you want to be technical about it, we're all aliens choosing to incarnate as human beings.

I can't say I've ever felt very human myself. I've never felt I've fitted in.

That's because you're coming from a very different perspective in regards to others. If what you believe doesn't match what most believe, at least not quite yet, then you will experience this feeling. Being human is simply being born into a human body and experiencing the myriad of amazing things there is on offer.

And, if you want to get technical about you, no, you're not human in spirit, but you certainly are human in body. This applies to many. There

> *are many souls who come as humans to help the race, and they do a lot to help. Such souls have been with us throughout history, and will continue to do so.*

This sounds like a complex subject with a lot more to it.

> *You could write a book on this subject; however this book will not be that one. Aliens, soul agendas and so forth are not strongly connected to empathy.*

Summary

- Some empaths feel like they don't belong in this world.
- This may be due to different perspectives from those around them, or that they feel separated from everyone.

Feeling Overwhelmed

Okay, the next sign is that you may feel overwhelmed at times. It may be from too many people around you or too many events occurring at once, but you may feel as though there is too much going on.

> *This is like information overload. In any case, it's an overload of too much energy and information coming in at once. The empath that does not filter out energies or is open to everything around them will certainly suffer from this.*
>
> *Once again, we return to the sponge analogy where too much psychic pollution is absorbed by the empath and they suffer from being flooded with energies that are not good for them.*

I find that having a shower makes a big difference to me. I always feel much better after it. I know grime doesn't bother a lot of people, but I can feel it clinging to me and I can't feel comfortable until I've rinsed it off.

I'm not sure why that is.

> *Some empaths are very sensitive to the vibrations of things. You generally will pick up the essence of things such as grime, and it doesn't resonate with your own energies. There is nothing wrong with this and you shouldn't*

have to apologize. If you work and operate better when you've had a shower, then so be it.

Water also has an energizing energy to it. It's one of life's energies flowing over your body and it helps cleanse your own energies.

Things such as incense, crystals, energized foods, and energized spaces can also help with cleansing and making you feel re-energized.

There are many methods; it's a matter of finding the ones that work for you.

It is important to ensure that if you do become overwhelmed, you take steps to clear the energies. If you are overloaded for too long, you will end up becoming fatigued, weary, or even ill.

Summary

- An empath can often feel overwhelmed with too much energy and become overloaded.
- This is due to absorbing too much negative energies.
- Water is a good cleanser, though there are other methods, too.

Another sign is that others consider you a highly sensitive person, and you are able to detect even small changes in energies, moods, attitudes, etc.

> *Most empaths are able to do this by their very nature. When it happens, it can make them feel quite uncomfortable, because they feel something has changed, but they do not understand the reason for it. It's always wise to follow your feelings. If you feel a break is needed from someone, or this is the time to retreat, then do so, but be diplomatic about it.*
>
> *As has been mentioned, you will pick up new information, which may change the entire equation. Trust in it, but it's also wise to give yourself time to attune and consolidate. Also remember, fear can taint such feelings, especially when you are attached to a particular outcome.*
>
> *This is why partners may become insecure as they feel something is wrong, and immediately believe it is something they have done.*

Summary

- Empaths can detect even small changes in energies.

- This may be in regard to someone's attitude changing or a situation having new factors in it.
- It is important for the empath not to automatically assume it's because of something they have done.

Buzzing in the Ears

Some empaths complain about buzzing in their ears. What is that all about?

> *Assuming that we're not referring to Tinnitus, which is a ringing in the ear that affects many people, they may be hearing spirits trying to communicate with them.*
>
> *The problem is that it doesn't work too well. Unless the spirit is perfectly attuned to the 3D level of vibration you are at, you will have difficulty hearing the message.*
>
> *This could be likened to inhaling helium, where the sound of voice comes out at a higher speed due to the way sound waves travel through the gas, making it higher and sound more comical.*
>
> *When a spirit attempts to speak in your ear, they are coming from a much higher vibrational level, and what you will pick up is a weird distortion that almost sounds like buzzing or a voice being played backwards at the wrong speed.*
>
> *Unless you can adjust your hearing, which, while not impossible, is rather difficult, it is unlikely you will pick up what is being said, and you will just hear an annoying noise.*

It's better if the entity just communicates telepathically, as language generally is not a barrier to understanding thoughts.

If you keep on hearing someone trying to talk to you, send a thought that you can't understand them and stop communicating in this matter. They may seek out another method of communication.

One of the things that I've noted over the years is that being an empath is only one part of someone's psychic abilities. It appears that when one is psychic, empathy is part and parcel of one's skills.

It is actually possible to be psychic without being empathic. Empathy is a connection to others and our oneness, but it does not automatically mean that you have other abilities, nor does it mean that those who are clairvoyant are empathic.

What you are observing is the many that are not only empathic, but also happen to have other gifts.

Such people have been referred to as Indigo or Crystal children, though they are now adults. More and more are appearing in this day and age.

This is not by chance. This is a period in our history where we get to experience such things without persecution or being condemned as witches or being in league with Satan. Though, make no mistake, people still will come from that school of thought. Still, it is possible to declare who you are and move onto higher levels of spirituality and abilities.

Empathy compliments other psychic powers and in many cases, enhances not only the skills, but also the results.

For instance, a psychic healer, who uses Reiki, or laying on of hands, will have their healing powers enhanced by empathy, as they will not only know what they need to do, but how and when.

Someone who is skilled in psychometry, which is the ability to read energy from objects, can also connect to the energy of any entities or elementals, which were or are attached to what they are probing. This helps give them a greater sense of what is happening.

Isn't that what psychometry is, anyway?

Generally, yes, but empathy enhances the effectiveness of that ability.

The point is, people have chosen empathy as a base skill, as this not only aids them on their spiritual path, but also aids them in whatever ability they have in addition to being an empath.

Remember, there is no shame in being psychic. There is no shame in being an empath. It does not make you a bad person or in league with evil.

It is just a tool, and how you decide to use it determines whether the experience is negative or positive for you and others.

Many people are desperate to hide that they are psychic and empathic. They wish that their powers would be taken away and call it a curse.

It is only a curse when you do not understand what is happening, and how you can use it to enhance your life.

Summary

- Some empaths may hear a buzzing or distortion in their ears.
- This may be due to someone trying to communicate with them from another level.
- Many empaths may have other psychic abilities.
- Such abilities can often be enhanced by being an empath.

This brings us to something that all empaths should be aware of. Not only can they pick up on what others are feeling, but they can actually change what others are feeling. Their very presence can be reassuring to another.

Here is a useful tip for those who sense negative energy. You can alter it by sending positive energy to it. Once you have worked out where the problem lies, you can lock in and heal it.

For instance, if you sense someone is in distress, send thoughts of healing, joy, and love their way, but make sure you do it without conditions. Just set the intention that those in distress will pick up on what they need to do, and take from it what they need.

This works for problems in your own life. If something is bothering you and causing you anxiety, focus on it, state that this is now healed, and move on.

There is no need to focus full time on such things. Just setting the intention, and holding the thought for a moment is enough. Then move on, and know that all will be as it needs to be.

I've found that I've been able to calm crying babies, with this type of technique, mostly on public transport, and I find that most of the time it seems to work almost immediately.

I will just focus on the child and send it healing, calming thoughts of love.

> *Yes, unless the baby is in physical distress, the child will indeed pick up the soothing energies and find comfort in it.*
>
> *This works for most things. Bless something rather than damn it. Send blessings to all that you perceive as evil in this world. Send positive thoughts to your enemies and politicians. Send love to those who you are at war with.*
>
> *If everyone did this, it could change the world overnight and we would advance to a much more spiritual level, which would be both joyous and exciting.*
>
> *If you feel you don't have the right to use your power to influence others, then just remember this, every thought you think, and every feeling you feel, is already doing that. For every negative thought, you are adding to a growing pool of energy, and trust me when I say, it will eventually hit a critical mass, and manifest in some way.*

It may be manifest in natural disasters such as hurricanes, or manmade ones, such as terrorist attacks. It is a law of the universe that we reap what we sow, and what we reap is seven times what we sow.

So be the change you wish to be.

I've seen that quote a few times.

Yes, and it's an important quote which cannot be stressed enough. All that is, is because we manifest it. To change this world to how you wish to see it, change your behaviour accordingly.

Remember, there is no shame in being an empath. It need not be a curse, but a blessing, and a blessing to all.

Summary

- Empaths can empower other people to feel better.
- Sending positive energies to trouble spots can make a dramatic difference.
- Bless your enemies rather than damn them.

Energizing Food

One thing I've found important is that we should be aware of the energies food may carry.

> *In this world, you'll find that much of the food is tainted with negative energies. This might be from the meal prepared by someone in a bad mood, or from the fear and trauma from animals.*
>
> *Whenever we eat something, we not only ingest the nutrients, but also any chemicals and hormones that have been added to it.*
>
> *Most of these are not good for our body, and things are made worse because the food in this present day generally lacks the minerals that our body needs to stay healthy.*
>
> *Over a long term, this has major health repercussions, and the results show up in many ways.*
>
> *But, as stated, not only do we ingest food that is not healthy for us on a physical level, but we are also at risk on a psychic level.*
>
> *All the negative thoughts and emotions that may be in a piece of steak, for instance, will be transferred into your own energies.*

So people should be vegetarians?

I didn't say that. Even vegetables may have negative energies if they are grown in a non-organic way.

Ideally, everything should be grown in harmony with the spirit of the vegetable or animal.

In an ideal world that is in tune with nature the spirit of, let's say a cow, will inhabit its body with the intent of growing it as a good source. Then when the time comes, the spirit will leave the body, leaving a carcass ready for preparation.

This is the harmony that would not only produce a much healthier food, but also stop the abysmal treatment of how we raise the livestock for food.

And how would one do that? I can't see it happening.

No, not the way things are being done right now. When we come from fear and the need to control nature, rather than work with it, we produce some terrible results.

When one is tune with nature, and I'm talking about feeling and working with the devas and spirits that inhabit all things, then one knows what needs to be done.

Rather than trying to push nature in a direction that it does not wish to go, we work with her, and move in directions that will benefit both human kind and the natural world.

The day may well come where this will be considered a normal stream of thought, but right now, this world is a long way off that happening.

As I said: in an ideal world.

Still, there are things you can do, even in this particular day and age.

Bless your food and thank it before you eat it. Tell the spirit that you appreciate the gift it has given you and you will do your best to make sure it is not given in vain.

So like saying Grace at the table before eating?

With saying Grace, you are thanking God. I am suggesting that you also thank the food source itself, be it meat or vegetable. Believe me; it will make a very big difference.

Also, eat organic whenever you can.

Scientists have said there are no particular health benefits to eating organic.

Scientists say a lot of things, and often find a study to support their hypothesis. The important thing about organic food is what is not put into it. If you can avoid the chemicals, the hormones, and the terrible conditions some livestock is raised in, you avoid ingesting that into your body and your energies. Trust me when I say that over the long term, it will make a very big difference on your health.

The other thing that is worth doing is sending your blessings and energy to what you are about to eat.

Visualize it being filled with universal love and life-producing energies, and see any fear and negativity being washed away.

You can do this with just thought, or you can put your hand over the food or drink, and let the energy flow from there.

Even this simple act can make a very big difference.

Remember, even if it's just a sandwich or a cup of tea, if it wasn't made when the person was in a good mood, their energies will be transferred to it, and by eating it, you will be taking in those energies.

Bless all your food and drink, and you will reap long-term benefits from it.

Summary

- Food and drink can be blessed and energized to help remove negative energies and instill positive ones into it.
- It's best to avoid junk food as the energy is not in harmony with what we need.
- The empath can sense if food is good for them or not.

Someone Has to Take

One of the things that people on the spiritual path find difficult to do is to receive help, or receive payment or gifts for something they have done.

While there is nothing wrong with receiving help or payment, many people feel that it is a failing on their part when they allow it to happen.

Accepting help, for instance, may make you feel like you are weak, or not competent enough to deal with things on your own.

Accepting gifts or money might make you feel that it devalues your service to another, or perhaps you may feel that people will say: I knew it; he was after something all along.

This is not a productive way to be, and by blocking others from giving, you are also blocking yourself and the flow of energy.

When you allow someone to help you, or accept something they give in gratitude, you are allowing the person to demonstrate who they are.

If everyone gave, and no one took, then whom would we give to? Someone has to take.

But there is also a gift you give to others by allowing them to give. You are giving them the opportunity to experience who they are.

If they feel they are a healer, and you are sick, you are giving them that chance to show it to both of you.

The same goes for money, etc. You are allowing them to show you that they appreciate what you have done.

If you find it hard to take, then remember, the other person may find it just as hard to do so, too.

Another important thing is that if you offer a valuable service, people will often feel uncomfortable if they cannot give anything in return. In fact, they may stop coming to you completely because of it.

So let others give to you, and as long as the flow goes both ways, and all parties are happy, then it's all good.

This is nice and all, but there are plenty of users in the world who are more than happy to take without giving anything in return.

I'm not saying to allow others to use you, or give to those who only take; I'm stating that both parties should allow a flow to occur between them.

When one refuses to allow another to help or show appreciation, it creates an imbalance.

In other words, don't let fear decide your actions. See everything as an opportunity for another. That is your gift.

Doesn't that somehow change the relationship or corrupt the purity of it?

I thought I answered that. No, it doesn't. If you don't allow the flow to go both ways, you will end up with no relationship in the majority of cases.

We are all part of the same energy, and when you help another, and allow them to help you in return, you are expanding your sense of self, and you are also doing what we are here to do. Provide opportunities and contrasts for others.

Still, there are those who will abuse the good will of others.

You've got it round the wrong way. We are not talking about all give and no take to someone who is completely self-centered, we are talking about not allowing others to give. That is the difference.

I find this hard to do, in any case, but I take your point. So, what does this have to do with being an empath?

> *Many empaths are on the spiritual path, as has been stated, and many wish for others to be happy. They also believe that they must give of themselves unselfishly and without conditions. Ironically, when they refuse to allow others to give back, they are actually being conditional. I will help you only if you don't help me back.*
>
> *The master understands that this is not the way to spiritual growth. Allow the flow, and bless what comes your way.*

Summary

- In order for someone to give, someone has to also take.
- It's best to allow a flow of energy exchange when working with other people.
- There is no shame in letting someone give to you.

Putting Your Needs Last

Some of us are driven by a need to help humanity, and we never feel that we have done enough. This generally means that we take on much more than we should or more than what is healthy.

> *This is pretty much the same condition as the Centaury type person. Someone who doesn't know when to say 'enough', nor do they feel they can say 'no'.*
>
> *While it's commendable to want to help as many as you can, you are not doing yourself or them any favours if you allow yourself to burn out.*
>
> *There needs to be ground rules when you are taking on this type of work, especially if you are not charging for it.*
>
> *Rather than trying to fit in what you wish to do in between what others ask of you, you should create a space and time for when you help others and stick to it.*
>
> *For instance, give yourself one day a week where you do nothing but non-empath related activities and do not breach it, unless there is a true emergency. Send a holding message if needed back.*
>
> *Fact is, most things can wait.*

Everything is always an emergency it seems. Problem is that things don't run to my timetable. It's not like I can really plan such things.

No, but you can decide when you are going to look at things. Set a time when you know you will be free and have the energy to look at it, and stick to it.

It may be one hour a night. It may be one day a week. It doesn't really matter. Intention is the key, and when you set it, it makes it easier to handle the people who come to you for help.

It also helps when they know they will most likely get an answer, rather than wondering if you've forgotten about them.

In the meantime, make sure you look after yourself. Exhaustion leads to bad habits, and lack of proper food intake and exercise.

Understand that no one requires you to put yourself last. In fact, if they do, then they are the very people you should avoid helping, as they will mostly just drain you, and move on without a second thought.

There are many Lightworkers out there who allow themselves to become depleted. They often feel that if they can just do one more thing, they can rest, but there is always something else that comes along, be it work, family, friends, or people just looking for help.

While we are multi-dimensional beings, we are still restricted to one body in the three dimensional world. (Though is it normal to be incarnated in multiple bodies at the same time, you would not normally be aware of this.)

Look after yourself, and take the time you need. If the person truly needs helps right then and there, and you can't help, there will always be others who will step in. No prayer or call ever goes unanswered. (Though, the answerer often is ignored.)

Ignored in what way?

People often ask for help, but they have a specific idea on how that help will arrive. Often the aid they receive is not what they are expecting, so they decide to ignore it. This happens much more than you might believe.

This occurs because people sometimes don't want the answers; they just simply want validation of what they want to hear, which is often not what they need to hear.

If you send out a call for help, know that it will be answered, but keep yourself open to what comes along and understand that it may not always be to your liking. But it will be what you need to hear.

Summary

- Many empaths have a tendency to put themselves last, leading to exhaustion and burnout.
- It is advisable to set boundaries on your time usage and stick to it.

Shyness

I've noted that many empaths, especially the younger ones, are painfully shy. Is there any reason for this?

> *Being shy is often a lack of self-confidence. If the person is experiencing things they do not understand, or things they feel they will be mocked for, they will often feel very shy around others.*
>
> *This is certainly more common with teens, as they know everything there is to know about everything that is out there, and so are quick to put down anything that they have not come across, with their own opinions on the matter.*

That was irony, right?

> *Of course. Most teens' awareness isn't that high. They are very intelligent, still learning, and putting the pieces together, but they have not become fully aware on higher levels, as a general rule.*
>
> *Of course, this is not for all teenagers and really I'm just picking on them as an example. This can apply to any group of people, but it's just more prevalent in teens.*
>
> *The thing is, when someone is more aware on a higher level than those around them, they are often put down, made fun of, or just dismissed*

as being weird or being a freak. They may become the subject of gossip, (which the empath will always pick up on) and often any actions they do will have the worst interpretation put on it.

So, unless you are confident in the people around you, yes, you will be shy until you get to know and trust them.

It is also true that the older you get, the less shy you become, and the less you care about what others think. This is due to years of observation and experience, and the understanding that the calamities that you once thought were so important really had little bearing in the long term, nor does anyone really care about them. Fewer still remember them.

Shyness is just part of growing up and discovering yourself. The more comfortable you feel about who you are, the less shy you will be.

Is there anything that can be done to help shyness?

Bach Flower Remedies can assist. And not letting others put you down certainly helps, however it's easier said than done in a society that thrives on cutting down people. Still, if you stand firm in your own power, and who you are, it will help.

Results beget results. Most people actually are more focused about how others see them, in spite of what they might say, do, or judge about another. What they see is what they project.

High confidence projects, and belief in oneself (and there is no reason not to believe in yourself as we have the tools to do what we need to do) will create charisma. That is, others will sense your self-confidence and self-belief and react to it.

To some this comes naturally; to others it's often a battle, especially if they were put down by family member or peers.

Just remember, you are not your past; you are who you are being right now. Work with that, and results will follow.

Summary

- Many young empaths suffer from being shy.
- This is due to a lack of self-confidence.
- Be who you wish to be in the moment, and trust in your feelings.

Before I released this version of this document, I put it to the empath support group to ask any questions they would like answered. This section deals with those questions, which I have received. Names are used with permission.

Chemical Imbalances

Daniel asks:

Hi, I was wondering to what extent the physical body has on emotions and to what extent a person's chemical imbalance can cause negative or positive emotions. Obviously there is some connection here but I am interested in how our mind can counteract these feelings, and to what extent eating something healthy or thinking something positive can help.

> *This is a good question because the physical can have a dramatic effect on the emotions, especially if one is sensitive to energies.*
>
> *Food has a very large part of play in how we feel, as do our emotions. We've already covered these things, but it is worth repeating that bad food can make us feel terrible. As it is said, we are what we eat, and thus when we ingest weak food with negative energy, our bodies take this on. A change in our diet and ensuring that our body gets the building blocks it needs can have a dramatic effect on how we feel.*

The real question here, though, is can we overcome the imbalance with just the mind or will power. The answer is, unlikely.

If you are, for instance, a psychic sponge, a cleansing would be in order to start to heal.

Shock and trauma are at the basis of many imbalances, and they need to be dealt with, too.

Trying to just get over it does not work for two reasons. What you resist, persists, so using will power to overcome something is actually drawing it to you and giving it more energy.

The other reason is that though you may actually prevail, at least in the moment, it's a false victory, as you've not dealt with the causes.

I remember when I was depressed back in the 80s and 90s. I would feel fine one moment, and then, I would, for no apparent reason, feel myself slipping into anxiety and depression. Nothing I could do seemed to stop it. It was almost as though I could feel the energy slide down. It was very frustrating.

Yes, and this was because you came from a place of fear and anxiety and did not trust that things would work out fine in the end.

Fear is one of the primary causes of chemical imbalances. Stress is another, and both are dismissed as though they are not important, or as a sign of weakness on the part of the person who suffers from it.

I think stress is now starting to be recognized as a problem, though.

Yes, there are inroads being made to recognize that stress is a killer; however it's still not taken seriously enough as yet. As long as it's not costing anyone money, it will be continued to be ignored in the places where it's generated the most.

This is especially true of the work place. While you can't always avoid stress at home, work places almost specialize in making stress part and parcel of our working experience.

It can be likened to passive smoking. Not so long ago, smokers were free to chain smoke in the office, exposing non-smokers to their second hand fumes. This certainly wasn't healthy for anyone, but no one cared, even though they knew it was doing others damage.

At least no one cared until someone successfully sued for contracting lung cancer, I think it was, due to passive smoking. Then it all changed. I guess the moment someone manages to sue for stress, things will be done.

People have successfully done that already, but it's normally between the company and the plaintiff. And the conditions are that it must not be discussed outside of court.

Point is, though, that eventually, when it starts to actually cost businesses enough money due to lost productivity, and they are made accountable for the conditions in their work places, then it will change.

The original point here was that in order to deal with chemicals imbalances, you must either treat the cause, or change your lifestyle, which can be pretty much the same thing.

The section on Bach Flower Remedies is invaluable for those who wish to treat such imbalances.

Summary

- Food plays a large part in how we feel.
- Fear and stress may cause chemical imbalances.
- Finding the cause of the imbalance and treating it is important. Also changing your lifestyle may assist.

Dealing with Sociopaths

I've had a few people ask about how an empath deals with a sociopath. To be honest, I'm not even quite sure what that is.

> *Are you sure they are talking about sociopaths because, by definition, they are people who have no empathic connections and will use other people to get what they want at their expense?*

Well, that's what I'm being told.

> *Okay, for the sake of this argument, we'll say it's a sociopath they are dealing with. If it's in the work place, then they can be a problem as they tend to drain every resource in order to get their own way.*
>
> *If the empath is trying to do the best they can to be helpful, they can be abused and used. It's not just the empath who would be vulnerable, though. Many people are subject to the machinations of a sociopath.*
>
> *The real question here is: Why would you allow it to happen? The answer generally is: Fear.*
>
> *Fear of offending. Fear of getting fired. Fear of retribution. Fear that they may be the ones in the wrong and just should try harder in order to make things better.*

> *Yes, under those circumstances, they will be drained, and it is understood that it may not always appear practical to escape the sociopath's sphere of influence.*

If I think about it, I'm pretty sure I worked for four years under such a person. In all honesty, I couldn't see any way out of it.

> *They needed you more than you needed them. You could have just said no to some of the unreasonable demands, or stood your ground. However, your circumstances are rarely ever normal, and there were other forces at play there, which you have since countered and removed.*
>
> *However, your circumstances can hardly be said to apply to the general populous, and so let us look at some of the ways they can avoid being drained by such people.*
>
> *First off, it needs to be understood that nothing is random, and that we are living in both a reality of our making and a co-created reality.*
>
> *This means that you are in a situation that you have agreed to. As the soul is rarely frivolous, you will find that there is always a reason as to why this has manifested as such.*

This argument has been used many times, but it really doesn't work as it comes across as both insensitive and simplistic.

> *It is not until you acknowledge where you are and your part in it that you can start to change anything. If you decide you are a victim, and everything is out of your control, then that is the reality you are choosing for yourself. You can argue that this is not the case, but you can't have free will if you are put in situations not of your choosing.*

Many people would disagree.

> *Indeed they would, and as a result remain stuck in their current situations. Why they would choose to do so is known only to them and their higher self. However, if they decided they have had enough, then they will seek out answers, and if they are serious about changing things, then they will start to change the way they think and their belief system.*
>
> *Remember, your reality is based on your belief system, and while being a victim can be a very seductive thing, in the end, it is a choice that you have made on some level.*
>
> *Honestly, you asked me how to deal with being drained by a sociopath. The answer is that until you understand that you are there by your own design, then nothing is going to*

change, or if it does change, it may not be the results you desire.

Okay. So we are there by our own design. How does this help?

First of all, by taking responsibility for where you are at in your life, you can then sow the seeds of a new situation - one that does not have negative people around you. But be warned, unless you happen to be a master at manifestation, it may take a while for things to change. The key is always choosing the same thing, over and over again, and stating 'this or something better'. Better being a relative term, of course.

Empaths are often subject to being abused by many types of people. There are the ones who gain their energy through intimidation or domination. There are those who manipulate through guilt, and those who coerce others into doing their will.

Now, you can argue that you never intended to be subject to such people, or that someone, like a child, is too young to have created their situation, and once again, I would beg to differ.

We are not born to random parents. The soul aspect is very much aware of the choices they make before being born into this life. Sometimes things don't go the way they choose, and so they shift to another reality where they do get to experience what they desire.

To some, this may appear as the death of the person, but it is often the case that the soul has shifted to another timeline (which might be said to be parallel) to continue on in their mission and goals.

If you do not wish to be here, you simply wouldn't be here. You would be somewhere else.

In this point, you would need to bear in mind that you are in a situation that is happening because you, on some level, desire it to be.

So, let's say you accept this universal law, and you understand that you no longer wish to be subject to people who use or abuse you.

First of all, understand that these people have given you valuable insight about who you are, your nature, and perspectives that you may not otherwise have gained.

They may have made you stronger, made you aware of what you are capable of, or trained your endurance for coping with strenuous situations or circumstances.

Of course, this is often very difficult to see or understand until you are looking at it in retrospect. Nothing in your life is for the worst, not in the long run. When we see others as victims, we are doing them a great disservice.

Tell that to someone who has been molested as a child.

I'm not saying that there shouldn't be compassion or acknowledgement, and really, if you want to get into this subject, you can get very deep into what is really going on.

Suffice it to say that such things are symptomatic of the society we live in, and we should seek to redefine who we are so such situations to not occur. For now, though, we need to stick to the subject at hand.

Okay, so we acknowledge the part they have played in our lives, then?

Yes. Thank them and bless them. Then decide where you wish to go from this point. Generally, there are two things to this. The circumstance will resolve itself when you've done what is needed to make the situation change.

People who are stuck in the same drama over and over again are those who, instead of trying to work out what will end it, will perpetuate it by being the victim in it. In that case, they will find it difficult to cope in the long run and become very drained and exhausted.

However, if they shift and decide enough is enough, the people who are creating the difficulties in their lives will be either removed, or they will shift themselves, and no longer be a problem for the subject.

The other thing is that new situations will arise for you. You may be prompted to leave the job. Circumstances may change around you, and you will no longer be subjected to the sociopath. It may be the most unexpected thing that occurs, but the results will be that you will move on.

What about those who have them in their family, or as their partner?

Family can be tricky, as many people are reluctant to cut them out of their life. Yet, in the end, that may be the only option. You cannot cure them, as they don't see themselves as having a problem, at least, not when they are getting their own way, which they normally do.

Partners can be just as tricky, as they don't let you go easily. The sociopath wants their cake and to eat it too, so to speak.

For the empath, living with a sociopath is something they should avoid as they will always experience drama and frustration. Things only become better for a short while when there is an ultimatum laid down.

In the end, the best choice is to leave, and once again it's choosing to create the reality. It may eventually cause a massive shift. But the reality will eventually be created, and you will no longer have the person in your life.

This is stating it simplistically, but suffice it to say that there is much more to this mechanically than what we are discussing here.

Some people say that they find being in the presence of a sociopath actually less stressful as they don't pick up as much from them.

A sociopath holds his cards close to his chest. Some may be seen as straight shooters, but believe me, they have their own agendas very well hidden.

In this case, they don't send out as much energy, so there isn't as much to pick up. Yes, it's possible to have a break by connecting to them, but I wouldn't recommend it as a healthy alternative.

Okay, so any more to be said on this subject?

> *Just that sociopaths have their purpose. Once they have served them, bless them, thank them, and move onto the next phase of your evolution.*

Summary

- Sociopaths have little empathy. They don't send as much information out, so an empath will not pick up as much.
- They serve a purpose in our lives, and when that is done, it's time to move on.
- We are here of our own choice, so when we are ready, we can choose a new reality without the sociopath in it.

Narcissists

A narcissist is someone who is self-absorbed. They may be any gender or any age. They are different to sociopaths, though they may act in the same type of manner.

The biggest difference is that a sociopath, but definition, does not have any empathy, but they may seem like they do as they are masters at mirroring people and telling someone what they want to hear.

While it's possible that a sociopath can also be a narcissist, a narcissist can also be an empath.

This confuses a lot of people as it's assumed that an empath is contrary to being a narcissist, however this is not the case.

An Empath Narcissist is someone who has a big investment in their ego. They will work hard to always be right, even if they are wrong and if you call them on this, they will flat out deny they have made any mistakes, even if you quote their own words back to them right away.

They also have a tendency to not listen to advice, often going ahead and doing their own thing, even after they have been told to stay out of a situation or that something is a really bad idea.

Their main problem is their ego and the need to be seen as always being right. This generally stems from a critical childhood where they were always put down or told they were not good or clever enough.

> *You'll find that narcissists are often broken people who never got the attention or love they needed when growing up. That's not to say that all never got it. Sometimes it may be due to being spoilt rotten and always getting their way.*
>
> *However, when a narcissist happens to be an Empath, that's a strong sign that they had a traumatic childhood.*

Some people argue that an Empath can't be a narcissist because if they truly are an empath, then they would not do the things they do.

> *That's akin to saying that all psychics are spiritual. Fact is, they are not, and not all empaths fall into the stereotype of being compassionate, selfless beings.*
>
> *In fact, it's a dangerous assumption that this is so because more often than not, it's not true.*
>
> *Empathy does not make one good or bad or better, it simply is an ability you may have. What you do with it and who you decide to be is what counts.*

Well, there is the argument that an empath can't hurt another because they will feel it themselves.

Not all empaths. Some, yes, for sure. Some are very advanced. But some just are able to feel what others are feeling and not be affected. It's not unusual to see an empath who will use and abuse their abilities for self-gain.

This is common with friends and family. Take the mother who guilts their children or partner into doing what they want. They certainly may be an empath, but their need to have attention focused on them and have their ego sated will override any concerns about the effects their actions will have on others.

Now, that's not to say that there won't be moments where they won't care, but don't assume that being an empath means you are somehow immune from negative actions.

So, any advice on how to deal with a narcissist?

Well, don't bother to argue for a start. There is no point. Just nod and go ahead and do your own thing. If they demand attention, then give them some. It often doesn't take much. But don't let them control or drain you.

That sounds like you're condoning their actions.

If it's family, then you are working to get them to a point where they can listen to you. Until they feel they have been heard, then that isn't going to happen. Remember, most Empath

> *Narcissists need healing and that can only take place when they are in a receptive space.*
>
> *If it's someone who you don't have to have in your life, then ask yourself why you are putting up with them? Call forth someone who isn't a drain. After all, what benefits do you really gain from such a relationship?*

Well, easier said than done at times, no?

> *Depends on what you want. If you want non-toxic relationships, then set your boundaries and call them forth to you. They will come. Don't stay with someone just out of fear. That's not living a healthy life.*

I still feel you're missing something here.

> *If it's family, then they need healing. You can't heal someone until they are in a space to accept it. If it's not family, then you need to decide if you want to go down the healing path or if you're happy with how things are. If you're not, then move on.*
>
> *Of course, some narcissist can't be dealt with. Some are actually sociopaths and that's a terrible combination. In which case, you really are better to just cut them out of your life if you can.*

Once again, easier said than done.

Only if you don't believe in free will. We always have a choice. We might not like how things turn out initially, but they will always work out for the best. Don't give your power away to others. As is said, even not making a choice is making one.

> *Yes, you will need to take responsibility for your part in this but consider this: Maybe that is the lesson or experience to be gained here. Learning how to deal with such people.*

Summary

- A narcissist may also be an empath
- They may be borne due to lack of attention, love or trauma.
- If they are important to you, give them what they need so they can be receptive to healing.
- If they are toxic or destructive, then break ties with them as soon as you can.

Using Drugs and Alcohol

Gina Thompson asked:

Can you include as to why empaths always end up using alcohol and/or drugs to turn down their sensitivity?

> *I wouldn't suggest that they always end up doing so. Some actually don't ever touch such things as drugs or alcohol because they know that they would not like the consequences.*
>
> *Let us ask why some empaths turn to drugs and alcohol to dull the pain.*
>
> *This is due to the fact that many just can't cope with the reality they are in. They pick up so much trauma and hurt around them and they have no coping mechanism in place. So they turn to something that they feel will numb the feelings they are being overwhelmed with.*
>
> *Of course, you don't need to be an empath to do this. Many non-empaths will do the same thing.*

Personally, I've always felt that drugs and alcohol are pretty useless as the problem will still be there in the morning. I always preferred to spend my time finding the solutions.

> *True, and you will know it wasn't a pleasant experience. Sometimes you barely survived. Many empaths feel they won't survive unless*

they do something that blocks the pain. Does it help them? In the very short-term, they will find relief, but such activities have their own issues. We don't need to go into what they are here because they are well documented.

If you are able to avoid drugs and alcohol, as an empath, it is wise to do so. You will not be doing yourself any favours by indulging in them.

I will also mention that in spite of the short-term relief they may feel, drugs and alcohol can make the empath worse. They become much more vulnerable to the energies around them, and in many cases, their spirit is forced into the astral world, which may leave them very vulnerable to attacks.

This is also true if you are doing it for recreational purposes. Anything that alters your vibrational levels may have a devastating impact on both the body and the soul.

The soul cannot be hurt as such, but the body will suffer, especially for repeated use.

Once again, it's a choice. Is this what you wish to do, and where you wish to go? Does it serve your purpose, especially in the long-term? Is this how you wish to be remembered?

Summary

- Empaths use drugs and alcohol to avoid the pain they feel.
- This can make things worse for them in the long run as it may force the soul out of the body, leaving them more vulnerable to the energies out there.

War and the Empath

Derech asked:

Do you have any insights or advice on how to deal with the impact and effects of terror and war for an empath?

I am extremely empathic and lived in Israel for seven years. I am currently based in the US, but even with the distance I am in a complete 'frozen' state today with what's happening right now.

How can an empath deal with these effects, especially when friends and loved ones are in the midst of it. I know this is a challenge for anybody to deal with, but as an empath - it feels even more overwhelming.

Any insights are appreciated.

> *Hi, Derech, war is traumatic by nature. It is a symptom of the insanity of the belief systems that are part of the make-up of cultures and religions, and yet it will resolve nothing in the long-term.*
>
> *Not only are the people involved sending out fear, hate, and terror, but the land itself becomes saturated with it.*
>
> *Any empath who goes to a war-torn zone, or to a land that was such a zone, will pick up very*

strong feelings of the terrible things that happened there.

Both the land and the people need healing.

You cannot stop war until people change their core belief system and stop seeing themselves as separate from others.

The terror that you experience are your chakras being stuck wide open and frozen with trauma. Mixed in there is frustration, anger, and disbelief that these things can happen as they do.

One solution is using the Bach Flower Remedies. Star of Bethlehem would be a must, as it helps clear the trauma. Rock Rose will help you deal with the terror, and Holly will help with feelings of anger and frustration. Red Chestnut will help with the fear you have for your loved ones, and Gentian helps with knowing that all is as it should be, in spite of contrary appearances.

If people go together and send healing thoughts of love and healing to such places, you would start to see a shift. However, too many have too much invested in the drama, or have vested interests in things remaining that way.

Still, the time will come when there are enough of us to make a difference. Even now, there is a growing movement, but it is far from complete. But differences have been made because of it.

You once told me that war is useless because eventually those you repressed or eliminated will return to plague you.

If you know that death is just a transition, and that the only way to resolve a war is with both parties coming to a peaceful resolution, then yes, you will know that war, in the end, is completely futile.

You may destroy your enemies now, but be rest assured that they will be back to trouble you, if not this lifetime, then most certainly in other lifetimes.

You may ask, well, if it's another lifetime, then why worry about it today?

This is akin to saying, I don't have to pay anything on my credit card for 4 years, so why not spend up and enjoy?

The time will come, and by soul and karmic bonds, you will be present in order to resolve it. You might feel that it's not going to be something you, personally, need to worry about, but you will not feel that way at the time.

Indeed, if something is happening in this lifetime, chances are it's due to an earlier conflict. Ironically, you would have felt in that life that you would not have to worry about it anymore, but here you are now, and having to deal with it.

Life is a continuum. The higher your awareness, the more you remember, and the more you start to understand that many conflicts are from previous lives and events.

People would do well to try to resolve any conflicts they have now because, until something is resolved, it will remain unresolved until such time that you resolve it.

Summary

- War causes trauma to both the land and the people in it.
- The trauma may cause your chakras to become stuck wide open, and leave you feeling traumatized and frozen by the feelings.
- Bach Flower Remedies can help.
- It is wise to resolve any conflicts you have in this life because they will just return to plague you at a later time.

Death and the Empath

Tell me about the empath and death.

You mean how the empath views death and how they are affected by it?

Yes.

When we are talking about death, it should be made clear that death is a transition from one state to another. Death does not mean you cease to exist.

What makes death so traumatic is the perception and illusion that those you love ceases to exist. What is left behind is a shell that once was animated by a soul. The body is no longer animated with the essence of that life.

For the empath, this will be traumatic on several levels.

If they were close to the departed soul, they will feel their energies still mixed in with departed one(s), and the shifting and breaking of energies will be extremely traumatic. This is the pain many loved ones feel when they are suddenly and often unexpectedly separated from their partner.

Also, they face a change in reality, which they are not prepared for. Their world is no longer balanced, nor is it making any sense. As much as they wish it to make sense, it won't, at least not right away.

Another level is the guilt that they often experience when someone departs. Even though there is nothing they could have done, many empaths feel responsible for when someone dies. How could they have stopped it? Should they have seen warning signs or had a feeling that something bad was about to go down?

This is especially true when suicide is involved, or if someone had a fatal accident. The 'what if's', and 'why didn't I?', and 'if only I had' thoughts come up and torment the mind and soul.

Then there is the pain of other people. For an empath, this is just as devastating as they are not only coping with their own pain and grief, but also from those around them.

This is also true for those who did not know the deceased. Going to a funeral for an empath can be quite traumatic as they can be bombarded with many feelings of loss and sorrow.

The reason why death is so hard in our current society is because we have it all tossed around, and the perspectives and understanding are often incorrect.

Death, as many know, and many more begin to know, does not exist. Nor do things such as accidents or untimely deaths truly exist.

The soul is never in the wrong place at the wrong time. It is never unaware of what is occurring from its astral levels.

The biggest question people face is 'why'? Why did they leave me? Why did this have to happen?

That's a reasonable question. I'm sure many have asked that and seen no rhyme or reason in many deaths. I know I'm left scratching my head about one or two.

That is because you do not know what was intended on a soul level, nor how one's passing will affect those left behind. There is a much bigger picture involved here. The very act of someone passing can spark events and changes that may not have happened otherwise or even prevent undesirable ones from occurring.

The people who are meant to be in your life, are in your life, and that is not by random chance. Whether they touch a life for a moment or a lifetime will depend on what is needed and agreed to.

Does that make the loss of a loved one any less painful? No, it doesn't. It takes a very high level of connection and psychic awareness for one not to feel that loss, and indeed, see it as an opportunity.

If you look back on the deaths you have had in your life, you'll see how vital they were to your own growth and your own path.

This I know, though I'm working to keep this useful for empaths in general.

It is an example. For many, death is often a catalyst for growth and awareness. They move into things that they were unlikely to do before.

There is also a belief that we must feel sad for the departed, otherwise we are a bad or uncaring person. If we do not mourn, or do not go through a certain period of time of grieving, then we may feel guilt over it.

Guilt is often a reason why we hang onto grief. We ask ourselves: how much did we really love this person if we can just move on without any sense of loss or pain. How will others view us if we are seen to 'not care'? How do we see ourselves if we find that we don't wish to suffer for the loss of another?

Yet, make no mistake; the departed does not need you to grieve for them. Once they reach the light, they are in bliss, and more often than not, the concerns of this world are left behind.

That does not mean they are forgotten, and when you call on your loved ones, they will come and leave many messages in many ways that they are there. Some even will manifest themselves so they can show the ones left behind that they are just fine, and they will look just beautiful.

They are fine. They are more than fine. They are home.

To those who have lost one dear to them, I promise you that you will see them again. You will be reunited, and if you both so choose, you will live more lives together for as long as you desire.

It's one thing to know this on an intellectual level, but how do you translate this to the emotional level? How do you bring comfort to those who have lost their loved ones? Saying that they aren't really gone doesn't seem to be all that useful.

As I said, it is natural to feel grief for the loss of someone dear. There is also a fear that your life may never be the same, and that you cannot cope without them. They may have been tremendous support, or loved you unconditionally, or they may have been the breadwinner.

Fear is one of those emotions that is intertwined with the sense of loss. Fear for the future, fear that they won't be able to cope alone or be capable of carrying on looking after family or children.

Death is not about the ones who have passed over, but those who are left behind.

So, how does the empath cope with death?

The key is shifting your understanding and perspective of death. Do not look upon it as something that should not have happened. If it was not meant to occur, then it would not have occurred. This does not mean you suddenly dismiss the pain, nor do you suddenly decide that it is irrelevant. It simply means that you are seeing things in a more holistic manner.

Those who you truly love will never truly leave you. They are there. They are by your side when you call, and they are helping you. You may not always feel them, but they are there.

The shift in understanding and perspective is key to coping with the sense of loss.

Do not harbour feelings of guilt of another's death.

Do not feel that your own life is ending because someone has departed.

> *Do not fear that you cannot cope. You will always have what you need to make it through, and indeed thrive.*
>
> *Life is about the growth and experience of the soul, and such things can be powerful catalysts.*

For my own comments, I've found that Bach Flower Remedies can be very comforting at a time like this.

For instance, Star of Bethlehem to help with the shock of a loved one's death.

Sweet Chestnut to help move from a place where you can't accept someone is gone.

Willow if you are feeling like a victim.

Pine if you carry any guilt.

Holly for the anger you may feel.

Vibrational Theory

This is something I worked on back in the mid-nineties, and it's something you wish to revisit for some reason?

> *Correct. We are going to discuss vibrations, and how they work and affect us. This is important information to be aware of, especially as empaths and psychics.*
>
> *I wanted to discuss it because it is important to understand how and why things work.*

Okay. So the premise of this topic is that everything is vibrational in nature.

> *Everything is vibration. This is accepted generally as a fact. Everything is made up of the same stuff, but how it vibrates and at what frequency determines what it is.*

Even emotions, such as love, fear, hate, etc.

> *Yes, and that's the basis behind the Bach Flower Remedies, though we'll not be discussing them in this section as it has its own for that.*
>
> *The reason it relates to empaths so much is because empaths can be particularly sensitive to the vibrations of other forms and matter.*

Thoughts are vibrations. Emotions are vibrations. Objects are vibrations. It's all real, and it exists at some level.

When I say it exists at some level, I mean it can be in thought, astrally, or dimensionally. Generally, though, thought creates, and that is normally the level things begin at, though not necessarily with us on this third dimension.

Some vibrations are not in harmony with other vibrations, so they may produce a discord, which can throw things out of balance and lead to undesired results, such as illnesses or negative emotions.

What we want to do here is look at the types of things that can affect us and what we should be aware of.

Okay, let's go through the list and look at things. Some of this will have been covered already, though.

This is so, but it's important enough to bear repeating.

Land Vibrations

Each land appears to have its own vibration.

For instance, the vibration of one country can be quite different from that of another country. A good example would be Holland compared to England, where the people and attitude seem to be very different to each other, or a country like Germany that is renowned for being neat and efficient.

Within the lands themselves, it is also common that the districts, and even small regions themselves, can hold their own individual vibration.

Some places appear to be naturally high in vibrations, such as Sedona in Arizona, and can certainly affect the people who visit there.

Other areas are said to be major earth chakras, such as Uluru, where the energy is said to be extremely high.

There are also places that are considered to be minor chakras.

A sensitive person can be driving along a road and sense the different energies of each place every minute or so.

Also, it's possible to walk into a house, shop, or building and sense how it feels. Some places might feel good while others might make your skin prickle, or you might break out into an uncomfortable sweat for no apparent reason.

> *This is actually not only due to location, but the spirit of the land itself. You may not be aware of this, but each object may have a spirit, energy, or entity attached to it.*
>
> *The Earth itself is said to have a spirit called Gaia, and this is actually true. Gaia might be said to be a collection of nature spirits, though it is a complete entity within its own right. The energy is feminine, hence we refer to her as 'she'.*
>
> *While Gaia may oversee the energy of the Earth, there are countless other nature spirits and entities that inhabit this planet. Who they are, and what they are depends on what they are trying to accomplish.*
>
> *Nature spirits have an agenda to not only manifest themselves in a perfect way, but to be part of the oneness they are aware of. Everything is connected, and nothing happens that does not have a reason for it.*
>
> *Nature has its own path, and humans, in spite of the appearance, cannot interfere with it.*

It is possible that those who try to dominate and subvert nature, and manipulate it to their own ends, will end up becoming separate from that energy.

To be very clear, not separate as in not being one, but they will not be in the presence of nature and the spirits that define it.

Nature will always manifest itself. It may not be where we are, but it will find the perfect place and do so.

When we travel from place to place, the sensitive person will pick up the energy of those spirits. They will also pick up any residual energy and past events, which are always present, even if the energy isn't strong any more.

When exposed for long periods of time, the vibrations of the area affect the people living there. Their energies start to match the energies of the land, and while each person has their own personalities, they will take on some of those qualities into the mix.

So, that would go for houses, parks, woods, plains, etc.

It does. It goes for everything. If you know of a high-energy area, it is beneficial to visit there.

You will generally find yourself infused with those vibrations, and it can have a very healing and energizing affect.

It's also important to stay away from areas that will drain you and bring you down.

Unless you are able to change the energy of that area, right?

Well, if you are strong enough, yes, you could, though you should ask yourself: is this what you should be doing? Remember, nothing is random, and those places exist for a reason. They may not be to your liking, but they have their purposes. Unless you are called to help, move onto a place that suits you better.

Family Vibrations

Family vibrations can be some of the strongest ones you'll have in your life. Giving birth, living with someone for many years, or just being under the dominance of another will often allow them to merge their energies with yours, which could give them some control over you.

This is also a product of soul groups.

And what exactly is a soul group?

A soul group could be anything that is a product of our soul aspect. In this case, it's when our soul aspect sends down two or more avatars to incarnate as human beings, though, this is not limited to just humans.

Generally, people refer to the main soul as their higher self. However, to call it the main soul would be to suggest that it's the soul at the top level. It is not. It is simply a level of soul, and it is part of a greater soul, and that soul is part of an even greater soul, and so on.

The same is true going the other way.

For the purpose of this exercise, we'll assume that it's the soul group that represents your family, though it's not unusual for friends and even those you don't know to be part of it.

The soul group is of a particular vibrational level, and all that comes from it will share the vibration at a base level.

In turn, it is possible for strong personalities to influence weaker ones, much like land can have a long-term effect on us.

Parents and Siblings

Well, let's look at parents then.

And we should also include siblings as a rule, because they will have the same base vibrational energy.

The empath can be very much at risk and have their energy and emotions manipulated by someone who matches theirs.

The typical example is the overbearing mother who uses guilt and emotional manipulation to get her children to do what they want.

Another example is the parent(s) who desire to mould their child into a mini version of them.

Great damage and trauma can be done to children who are subject to such manipulations, because they are much more vulnerable due to the energy they all share.

It's actually possible for one to implant an elemental into someone, giving them much stronger control over them.

Elementals, it should be mentioned, are...

Energy creations. They are also referred to as thought forms. They are non-physical (to us) and their function depends on what intentions and actions went into creating them.

If someone wishes to control you, and they focus on it long enough, they create an elemental energy, which can then be used (normally unwittingly) to complete the intended purpose.

Every thought contains energy, and that creates the thought form, which generally is very weak. When enough energy is used, it becomes more potent, eventually manifesting itself in a physical way.

It is a law that all elementals eventually return to the source, and subject the creator to the very energy they sent out. This is the law of Karma, or the law of cause and effect.

When someone intends to dominate another, and an elemental is created as a result, it normally can be resisted by the subject, if they do not resonate with it.

However, should there be something within that energy that already resonates with their own, then they are far more susceptible to it.

This is why parents and siblings can be much more effective at getting their own way.

Bach Flower Remedies can be used to dissolve such energies.

The empath needs to be aware of this vulnerability.

Such techniques of dominance should never be used with intention. Doing so will have grave consequences that may take lifetimes to resolve.

Drug Vibrations

A drug has its own vibration and by ingesting it, you are forcibly altering your own vibrations. While this might help some along the spiritual path, I also believe it locks people into a certain range of vibration which makes it very hard to transcend.

Drugs can limit you, but worse, they control you, rather than you controlling them.

It is true that people and mystics use them to gain certain awareness, and they may have great success in doing so. However, this is a form of a cheat and while producing the desired results, will not actually aid them in their soul agenda.

The key to spiritual growth is being, that is, being rather than doing. If you ingest drugs or alcohol, you are being that drug or beverage, and not coming from who you really are.

This is fine if you wish to experience what that is like, but do not be fooled into thinking that you're making true spiritual progress.

The adept will not need these things, and the master will be able to enter the desired state without said drug when needed.

So don't take drugs or get drunk?

It's a personal choice, but they are not empath friendly. In the end, you cannot escape what you are trying to escape from by using them. It does not work. All you are doing at best is putting things off, and they will come back to you, even if it's another lifetime.

It's a choice. Make the one that suits the future self you see yourself as.

Sexual Vibrations

In my experience, sex can be physical without any emotional or energy connection, or it can be a very powerful experience where both parties connect on a very intense level, almost to the point where the physical is almost transcended.

Also, from my observations (and experience) the latter type of sex can be used as a weapon to manipulate the other partner to get their own way.

That's certainly not news to the majority out there. Sex has been used as a tool and a weapon for as long as we've been around.

Like the family, people can use their energies to hook into another person, and really give them a hard time.

Sexual energy is very potent, but there is another level where the two (generally) souls merge, and their energy is as one.

This is fine as long as both parties are able to maintain their individual identities; however what normally happens is that they become lost in each other.

If one of the partners happens to be unstable, or self-destructive, they can drag the other down with them, creating a dangerous downward spiral, which can be very debilitating.

I once had that happen to me. It was as though all the energy had been sucked out of me and I could barely function.

It was because the energy was being drained out of you.

I was told at the time the way to fix this was by imagining a set of spiritual silver scissors and by cutting the links between me and the lady. I felt instant relief, almost as though something physical had been lifted.

Yes, you literally cut the energy cord that was draining you. It worked because you actually desired to be free. It wouldn't have worked if you had wanted to maintain the connection.

Why would I have wanted to do that?

People become lonely, fearful, or maybe addicted to the energies. They are afraid to let go. It's also a very destructive and negative state of being.

Once again, empaths are very susceptible to such things. Sexual energy is the stuff of life, it's who we are in the purest form, but on this level, it can be much misunderstood and misused.

So, avoid sex?

Of course not. Just be careful whom you engage in sex with. Make sure they complement not only your energies, but who you are, and where you are going, and vice-versa.

Relationship Vibrations

Often in the beginning of a relationship, we find pleasure by giving and bolstering another's energy.

Unfortunately, we tend to also disconnect ourselves from our own source and start to run out, especially if it's mainly a one-way street.

Some people are extremely adept at manipulating energies and synching them into the object of their desire. The target often feels an inexplicable pull towards the manipulator, though they had no idea why.

Breaking away from each other's energies can be a very painful process where you feel like you are being broken inside. Part of this pain can also be due to having to change your perceived reality to something completely different.

> *This goes back to the other topics, where someone will use their energies or create elementals to control you.*
>
> *The empath is very much at risk, because they have a very strong ability to change their own vibrational level to match that of another. Once they do that, either out of sympathy, or maybe a soul call, they can become vulnerable to such situations.*
>
> *Often, what happens here is that when a couple breaks up, only one person is disengaging from the energies and accepting a new reality. The other partner, though they will feel it, will be in*

> *denial, either out of fear or by hanging onto a belief system that no longer is valid for them.*

Which is also referred to in Bach Flower Remedy terms as the Sweet Chestnut state.

Healing Vibrations

Colour

Colours can be potent with healing. Each colour represents a vibration, and when a certain one is lacking, introducing that colour into a room, person, etc, will help bring balance.

> *Colours are very powerful. The right colour can bring balance and healing to a person, whereas the wrong one can actually aggravate and unsettle them. The aura is composed of many colours, and it is possible to heal a body by introducing the appropriate colour into the aura.*
>
> *This is because the aura reflects our current state of health. Our illnesses show up first on that level before on a physical level.*
>
> *Now not everyone can see the aura, but most can feel the energy, and an empath is certainly sensitive to it.*

> *If they go through the colours in their mind, they will feel which ones feel right and which ones don't.*

I guess that's why a good decorator will know which colour to use.

> *Only if they are in tune with those they are creating for. Otherwise, they tend to use what works for themselves.*

Clothes

Wearing certain clothes and different colours can have a profound effect on how you feel.

> *There is no denying that nice clothes will make you feel better, which is one reason why certain people have an addiction to buying something new every week. There is another level, however, that people don't normally take into account. Cut and colour can have a very profound effect on the energies you carry.*
>
> *The wrong type of article of clothing can actually make you feel worse, whereas the ones that compliment you and your energies will enhance it.*

I remember, back in high school, there was this brown jacket I would wear that would make me feel less coordinated. The effect was so blatant that I actually knew it was the jacket, and I stopped wearing it.

That jacket was a bad cut and the wrong colour, hence it was a double whammy. The point with clothing is that you should go with your feelings. Most females already know this, which is why they may take their time buying a new outfit. They understand the nuances and subtleties of outfits.

Vibrationally, what you put on your body is just as important as what you put in it.

Gemstones

Gems, rocks, and crystals carry their own individual vibration. When choosing them, ensure they feel good to hold. Some might prickle in your hand, so they may not be compatible with your energies.

Like flower remedies, gemstones, etc, carry their own vibrations. They can have an effect on how you feel. But, they must be attuned to you on some level, and you must be attuned to them. Some people will tell you that a gemstone must be first awakened before they work, but I also tell you that the right one will awaken naturally when the right person takes possession of it.

While it's reasonable to say that all gemstones and the like will produce a desired result, the effect many vary from individual to individual. It depends on where the person is spiritually, and how in tune they are with the energies.

Personally, I've not found them to really work for me. Back in the early '90s, I carried around a few to help me attract a partner, but they didn't seem to do anything.

Well, no, they wouldn't have. They weren't right for you, and attracting a partner wasn't part of your soul agenda at the point of time. The thing is that they don't actually make things happen, they are for support and enhancement of who you already are. It's true that some might awaken certain abilities, some may produce undesirable outcomes, and some will certainly make you feel very uncomfortable.

Gems, stones, and the like should be treated with respect, whether they resonate with you or not. There are often spirits attached to them. Also, it is unwise to sleep with them as they can disturb your energies while sleeping.

I know every time I've done that, I've awoken feeling quite uncomfortable and out of sorts.

> *You do not sleep well at the best of times, so unless there is a stone that specifically helps you to sleep, then you are best to avoid doing that.*

Flower Remedies

Flower Remedies are pure vibration. They are very potent in restoring links to your higher self. The trick is finding the right one to take, but once you've done that, the results are often miraculous.

They are also capable of dissolving vibrations that have been instilled in you by other more dominant forces.

Meditation Vibrations

There are certain mantras that we can say that are said to help in the meditation process. For instance, 'Om' is said to be the sound life makes.

By saying or thinking this mantra, you are introducing that vibration into your body, and you can create a resonance with those vibrations. The key is also intention. 'Om' without intention may not have as great an effect.

Each chakra has a mantra that actually matches the sound or resonance of it. By saying these mantras, you can help strengthen the vibrations.

In summary, be aware that everything is vibrational in nature. The empath should ideally keep that in mind as it can hold the key to why they are feeling or even acting in a certain way.

Soul Calls

Just to finish off this section of the book, I'm putting in what a soul call is. It's been mentioned previously, so here is a fuller explanation:

A soul call is a cry for help from one soul to another. It is a desire, a prayer, a request to the universe, to God, or whatever you have chosen to believe in, to bring aid and help deliver the caller from their current situation.

No prayer goes unanswered. (When you do pray, make sure you choose your words very carefully, and ask exactly for what you are after.) How they are answered does vary though. One way is by another person receiving a soul call.

Remember that nothing is random. There is a purpose to everything we have called into our lives, even if it does produce undesired results, or what has manifested does not suit your path. However, consciously or unconsciously, we do call it into our lives.

So it's important to make your every thought in line with what you wish.

Every action and word should reflect what you want to experience.

If you listen to people, you'd be surprised just how they are continuously making negative statements as if they are fact, and then finding that such statements produce that experience. And thus they reinforce a negative personal reality.

People will come to this realization in their own time, normally when they have become weary of the pain and dramas in their life. It is at that point where they send out a call for help.

Those who receive such a soul call will feel an irresistible pulling towards the caller. For some, it will be like they are falling in love. All they know and feel is this almost irresistible compulsion to contact the person and know as much about them as they can find out. It is very difficult to ignore as you will always find it pulling at you the moment you let your guard down.

Generally, opportunities will arise where the two people will meet, and situations tend to occur where the true nature of the call is revealed and the one called knows exactly what needs to be done.

Empaths may experience a lot of soul calls. This is especially true if they are on road to self-realization, and calls come to them, almost like missions.

How long do they take?

A soul call may vary in how long it takes to complete. It depends on if the person answering is aware and understands the nature of the call.

The call can be as simple as giving the right words at the right time, such as delivering a message. Or it can be helping someone get to a safe place in their life. It can be helping someone stop a psychic attack that is happening to them. Some may go on for years, while others may last mere moments.

It is also not uncommon to get more than one call at once.

What do I get out of answering a soul call?

There is an enormous amount of knowledge, experience and self-realization to be gained by answering a soul call. While you are helping the caller, you may discover things about yourself that you never knew or even suspected.

This is often an opportunity for growth and the outcomes can be beyond your wildest dreams.

I've also found that even if the soul call required giving financial assistance, I always had enough to do what was needed, and indeed, found that the resources would arrive just before the soul call did.

What a soul call is not:

Soul calls are basically asking the universe for help. If you try to use it to target a specific person, it doesn't tend to work. You cannot use it as a tool to manipulate others. You certainly cannot use it to make someone fall in love with you and even if you could, why would you want to manipulate someone in that way, especially if you truly did love them?

The person who answers is normally the person who is most qualified to help, even if they are not who or what you were expecting.

How do you know when it is necessary to contact a person by phone, etc.?

You will feel the pull. Normally it won't let you be until you make contact. Trusting your feelings is the key, even if they seem totally illogical and insane. The best way to explain your actions is to tell the person that you had a very strong feeling you needed to contact them, and you apologize if you are intruding.

How do you break the soul connection from a person that does not want to let go of the past or forgive?

I, myself, have used two main methods:

One is to use Bach Flower Remedies. Walnut is known as the link breaker.

Sweet Chestnut if you need to accept a new belief system that this person shouldn't be in your life. Pine if they are using guilt to make you stay connected. Red Chestnut if you are over concerned for them.

The other is visualizing the link between you both, and then using a spiritual silver scissors to cut it. This one worked quite strongly for me when someone had hooked into my energies one time.

Do all soul calls consists of bad news only?

No, not always. It can be also for people you are about to share an experience with or help shift to another level. If you wish to have more pleasant experiences, you can always state the intention to the universe (or whatever you believe in) and it will happen.

Part 2 - Bach Flower Remedies

This section contains a full examination of Bach Flower Remedies, what they are, how they work and which ones to use.

They will focus on the usefulness for Empaths and what they so in general.

I'm going to give these remedies their own section, as they have so many good qualities for the empath.

The following is a revision of my original document. As the remedies are discussed, I invite my guide to make any further comments or point out things I may have missed.

What are Bach Flower Remedies?

Flower Remedies are unique when it comes to tools for healing.

This is what they are not:

- They are not toxic.
- They are not addictive.
- They are not herbal.
- They are not similar to orthodox medicine.
- They are not homeopathic like tissue salts.
- They are not like aromatherapy (which are herbal in nature).

- They do not generally work on a physical level (though they can produce amazing healing effects on the body).

What they are:

Bach Flower Remedies are the vibrational essence of the plant, tree, or even rock. They are, in essence, a captured dewdrop that has been sitting in the morning sun and has absorbed all the energy from the source is it on.

They are water, infused with the vibration of the plant, tree, or rock, and preserved with alcohol.

Water is very programmable and has a tendency to take on properties of what it comes into contact with.

They were developed by Dr. Edward Bach, who was a Harley Street doctor who became disillusioned with the methods of orthodox medicine. He gave up his practice believing there had to be a more natural and effective way to heal people and spent the rest of his life developing the Bach Flower Remedies.

His philosophy was: Treat the patient, not the disease.

He spent much of his life discovering which remedies did what and developed the methods and a complete healing system before he died.

What he would have had to have gone through to do this, I would hate to think, for he would have had to experience each of the emotions in the extreme, and then find the remedy for it.

Words cannot convey my respect for this man.

How do they work?

Bach Flower Remedies work on a vibrational level. Those are the higher and subtler areas that generally get called our emotions. The remedies help heal, clarify, and bring a reassuring perspective.

You may be wondering how could they possibly work? Are they just a placebo or a scam? Surely something as simple as taking a few drops from a bottle can't possibly heal where other methods have failed? Are they too good to be true? Are we being suckered into believing they work when they don't?

Having used them since 1994, and having sent out literally thousands of bottles (at my own cost as I believe in them so much), I can report an amazingly high success rate for healing.

The trick is to know which one to take, and when.

Even though it is a very simple and effective healing system, knowing which of the thirty-eight remedies to take requires some mastery.

The theory behind them.

I asked my guides about how they worked, and received the following information:

Firstly, I am making the following assumptions that have been true for me.

We are all spiritual beings and each of us has what is called a *higher self.* (In some esoteric circles, this is referred to as the *Overself.*) Our higher self knows who we are, understands our oneness with all. All our life experiences and what we need to do to obtain them are within it.

My other assumption is that everything is vibration. The level of vibration depends on whether something is physical or nonphysical. (And physical is a relative term, depending on the current dimension we are living in.)

If all things are vibrational in nature, then it follows that this includes your emotions, thoughts, and feelings. For instance, guilt would have its own vibrational frequency. When we experience guilt, we are not getting messages clearly from our higher self. The link between us and it is broken. The Bach Flower Remedy, Pine, will restore that link, and allow us to heal our guilt.

Radio station

You can liken your higher self to a radio transmitter that sends all the information you need for life. Even though it may be sending all the time, if the receiver (you) gets off frequency, or something interferes with that signal, you no longer are getting the instructions clearly if at all.

There are many causes for this to occur, such as shock, trauma, or any number of things that are part of daily life.

Each remedy is the exact frequency as that of your emotion or feeling. So taking pine, in regards to guilt, would be ingesting the exact vibration needed to restore the connection, and the feelings of guilt will no longer have any power over you.

Nature's fuse box

Another way of looking at it is that your connections to your higher self are like a fuse box with thirty-eight fuses. If all fuses are working, then all the connections are working. But if a fuse blows, then the messages you should be getting for that emotion are interrupted. The specific remedy replaces the fuse. It is also possible that more than one fuse might be blown.

This also explains why taking the remedies to prevent feeling a certain way does not work, as replacing a working fuse with a working fuse will not cause it to work any better.

Those clinical trials

It's noted that clinical trials were done to try to establish if the remedies were indeed effective. The conclusion was that, though harmless, they were no more effective than a placebo.

As I do not know how these trials were done, I can't comment on them. However, I can make the following observations:

If you use the wrong remedy by misdiagnosing the cause of the condition, then there will be no effect. While it's true that the power of our mind can produce healing, it does not necessarily follow that the remedies have no healing powers.

If they were just a placebo, then the ones I took to cure my life-long depression should have worked. They didn't. This was because I didn't address the cause of it. One day I had a flash of insight, and took Star of Bethlehem, which heals shock and trauma. There was a profound and immediate shift, and a lifetime of depression lifted and did not return.

If they were a placebo, then they would not likely work on plants and animals, and they certainly do work on them, though, once again, knowing which one to give is the key.

The easiest way to see results on a physical level is with the Bach Flower Rescue Cream. If you receive a burn, putting this on will heal it extremely quickly, and neutralize the pain. It also prevents any scaring. I've seen this on oil burns and when I have burned myself.

Sometimes, people will get a rash when using the cream. This is due to toxins being released, and it will disappear. Nothing can come out that wasn't already there to begin with. This is said to be a rare occurrence, though.

Having tried just about everything I could get my hands on from the time I could afford to (since the early 1980s), the Bach Flower Remedies are the only tool I have used consistently since I started using them in 1994, and with consistent success.

As said, and this bears repeating because it's very important, though they are a very simple system of healing, knowing which ones to use can take some mastery.

I believe that Bach Flower Remedies are an empath's best friend.

The goals with this section are to help provide what remedies are useful for which emotions and circumstances.

The problem with Bach Flower Remedies is that they are so simple in concept and use, that people just can't believe that they can possibly work and tend to dismiss them as a placebo.

What needs to be remembered is that simple does not mean useless. Simple is powerful, and all complex systems are built on simple ones.

Alcohol warning

The only caution that needs to be said about BFR is that they are preserved in an alcoholic solution. This can present a problem for those who are alcoholic, those whose religions forbid alcohol, or for children, whom you may not wish to give alcohol to, even if it's just a couple of drops.

You can get around these problems by:

- Mixing two drops into a dropper bottle of water, and then administering 4 drops of that dropper bottle into a glass. The potency is said to be the same.
- You can rub the remedies on temples or wrists.
- Some companies have an alcohol-free version of the remedies.

Taste

People often will report a strong taste when taking the remedies. Some will report a very strong tingling, almost like putting a very fizzy sweet on your tongue.

The stronger the need for the remedy, the stronger the sensation or taste.

People find that taking remedies that they don't need will have little or no taste or effect.

You cannot overdose with flower remedies.

Because of their nature, it's impossible to take too much. It's also not possible to become addicted. In fact, the opposite is true. The need for them lessens as you are cured. Eventually, you will forget to take them.

The kit

There are 38 remedies in all, each one of them having a different function. They also work on many levels. Each remedy may have more than one function.

Those thirty-eight remedies have been said to cover the entire range of emotions.

If you master all the remedies, you'll also have a much greater understanding into human nature and psychology.

Bach Flower Remedies and Elemental Energies

This is an area, which I don't believe has been dealt with before in regards to Bach Flower Remedies. As it is, it's still a theory; however I suspect there is truth to it.

As already explained, everything is vibration and energy. When enough creative energy is given to a thought or idea, it will become manifest on some level.

Nonphysical creations are called elementals or thought forms, and their sole purpose is to create the conditions that resonate with it in order to sustain itself. All elementals will return to the source eventually, as a rule, seven times stronger, and manifest itself in the creator's life.

This is said to be how the Law of Karma works, and why what you do returns to you in time, negative or positive. Intention is certainly the key here.

The reason for this short lesson is that I believe that every type of elemental energy exists on some level, and that includes emotions.

To the empath, being a psychic sponge leaves them open and vulnerable to other people's emotions, even if they are not fully resonating on those levels themselves.

If your parents had a very strong trait, as a child you may well have absorbed that energy, and while you may not act upon it, it remains within you. It possibly may have an effect on you emotionally and on who you are. It may even make you more sensitive to the same emotions in other people.

With this theory in mind, I believe that Bach Flower Remedies can help dissolve those energies and free the empath from strong emotions that they don't normally resonate with.

For example, if one of your parents was an intimidator, you may well find that you react to other intimidators in a much stronger way than others. I think such things are also the cause of triggers in people, where it doesn't take much to set them off because the energy has already reached a critical mass.

As you're reading about each remedy, also hold in mind the people you have been close with, see if that type also fits them, and see if they trigger you. If they do, then taking the relevant remedy might help bring relief and stop such things having power over you.

How are they made?

There are two methods:

The Sun Method. This method involves putting the flowers into a bowl of spring or well water, and putting it in the sun during a good sunny day.

The Boiling Method. Simply put, the flowers are boiled in a saucepan.

Of course, there are specific procedures for each remedy, but those are the two ways of doing it. It should also be noted that conditions have to be exactly right in order to obtain the proper result. The time of year, the plant in question, the weather, and so on, should all be perfect.

Anyone who makes them in their backyard without first studying how, should be considered as suspect. (Of course, they might be working on guidance, but there are many who do not seem to be!)

For those who want more information, the book *The Bach Flower Remedies - Illustrations and Preparations* by Nora Weeks and Victor Bullen contains full details on making the remedies.

How do I take them?

This is very important. Most people don't take the remedies correctly and then wonder why they don't get results. At the very least, when starting out, two drops should be taken at least four times a day.

What I have observed over the years is that the more you take the remedies, the quicker the results. It seems you become attuned to them, and where results might have once taken days or weeks, the same outcome can be achieved in a matter of minutes.

There are several ways of taking the remedies:

Definitions:

Stock Bottle: The bottle that the Bach Flower Remedy comes in. It normally bears the Bach label. There are some good quality copies on the market, however.

Stock Bottle

- Two drops directly from the stock bottle
- Two drops mixed into a glass of water and sipped at regular intervals.
- Two drops mixed into a 30ml dropper bottle and then four drops taken at least four times a day.

- Two drops mixed into a small spray bottle of water and used frequently.

Dropper Bottle: An empty bottle that is normally 30 ml or 1 fluid Oz.

Dropper Bottle

It is said that you should take the drops upon rising and before sleep. The minimum should be four times a day, though you can take them as often as you want or feel the need to. I recommend taking them whenever the state of mind you are treating comes up, which can be as often as every few minutes at the initial stages.

How else can I take them?

I've noted good results when I apply the drops directly from the stock bottle onto the wrists. There is no doubt there are other places where they will work, too. This is a good alternative if the patient is unable to ingest the remedies.

Taking them under the tongue.

Some people say we should take them under the tongue because it allows the body to absorb them faster. This would be fine if the remedies worked on a physical level, but as they are vibrational in nature, taking them under the tongue will not help. If you take them orally, always put them on the tongue.

Affirmations

Positive affirmations tend to come across as cliché nowadays. However, we are always creating with our words and intent, so saying an affirmation after taking a remedy will most certainly help the healing along.

Some practitioners use more than 2 drops!

There are some healers who use various methods of finding out how many drops they need to put into your bottle. I've had up to 11 drops from a remedy put in. The fact is, though, 11 will do the exact same job as 2. If someone insists that you need more, I would call into question their source and knowledge and grab my money and run.

Why don't they work for some people?

When taking the remedies, it's worth noting that one should have either a neutral or a positive attitude towards them. A deliberate negative attitude will block the effects, as with anything, even with orthodox medicine. We get what we ask for, and when one is being deliberately negative, you are asking not to be healed.

The other reason is that the actual cause has been misdiagnosed. This is surprisingly easy to do as our emotions are very complex.

For instance, I treated someone who had just lost her dog, and I used the obvious remedies, such as Star of Bethlehem and Sweet Chestnut, but didn't get the desired results. Then I noticed that she was trying to be brave, and not bother anyone, which is an Agrimony state. I gave her a couple of drops of that remedy, and the results were quite dramatic.

Knowing the remedies and what they do helps enormously.

I've got a friend who could use them, but they don't want to. What can I do?

Many people aren't ready to let go of their states of mind, dramas, and illnesses. They feel they will be giving up something, and in many cases they are right.

Maybe people don't want to give up their dramas because they feel life will be boring, and if things stop happening to them, then what will they use to justify to others that their life is hard and unpleasant.

Another example is that a person may come down with a cold because they need a break from something, such as their job, from which they are way too busy to take one. However, if they were to get sick, who could blame them for having to take time off, least of all themselves.

More than not, we are caught in an illusion that we need certain things for us to maintain our lifestyle, and we rarely give ourselves the space to step back and look at things from an outside perspective.

I'm a great believer of this world being just an illusion we use to experience who we are as put forth by the Conversations with God series. I also believe that very often we lose control of what we are doing and forget the illusion we are living in, making it a reality we are trapped in. When you are at that stage, it can be very hard to step outside and look at things. Also it can be very easy to fall back into patterns as soon as stress starts up again.

From self-observation, I have noted that there are times (even now) where I will fall into a poor me or victim drama, in spite of knowing better. Taking the remedies helps bring me back out of it, but it's very easy to fall into. There are even times when I want to be indignant, angry, or self-righteous about things.

I've got a few friends who would definitely benefit from taking the remedies, but I can't even get them to talk about it.

It seems that most enjoy their dramas and are reluctant to let go of them.

It's a conscious choice. Once you've chosen another way, then the tools will appear to make that a reality.

The decision must be made by the individual to heal. You can even cure someone, but unless you've actually 'plugged up the holes', they will eventually sicken once more.

I don't believe that there are any wrong choices, just things that don't suit your purposes.

What if I try to slip them into their drink?

You can do that. Many practitioners even suggest it. My point of view on this is that nothing can happen to someone without their consent on some level. Also, as I said, the healing would only be of a temporary nature if the person doesn't wish to be healed. The best guide you have is your feelings. If it doesn't feel right, don't do it.

Where do I get the Bach Flower Remedies?

One of the most common questions I get is: where do I find these remedies?

The answer varies from country to country. If you're in England, the home of the Bach Flower Remedies, they should be easy to find.

In Australia, they are sold not only in health food stores, but also in some pharmacies.

In most places, you will find them in health food shops.

As a general rule, buying Bach Flower Remedies is cheaper when it's from the U.K. This is because they are made there. It is normally cheaper to buy several, and even when you add on the cost of postage, it will work out for a much better buy.

My preferred source for a number of years has been from Skylark Books, who supply the Healingherb brand. I find these to be high quality and very effective.

Their website is at www.skylarkbooks.co.uk

What about the other remedies that are out there?

There are more and more remedies being discovered all the time. Two of note are the California Remedies and the Australian Bush Flower ones.

I've tried the California ones, and have felt little or no effect. That's not to say they don't work, just that they didn't work for me.

I tried a bottle of Australian Bush Essences. I used the entire bottle and found no effect on the desired condition. Whether it was too many remedies mixed in, or they just don't do what they are said to do, they simply didn't work for me.

I'm not really sure why people are working to discover more and more remedies. The Bach Flower kit is complete. It covers every known state of mind. The plants, trees, etc. used to create them, were specifically chosen for their non-toxicity. I'm far from convinced that these new remedies are needed or useful, or are even what they say they are. I feel they might even hurt an already proven, safe system.

Dr. Edward Bach wrote this before he died:

Attempted distortion is a far greater weapon than attempted destruction... mankind must always have a choice. As soon as a teacher has given his work to the world, a contorted version of the same must arise - the contortion must be raised for people to be able to choose between the gold and the dross.

'Random' Thoughts

When you take a remedy, it's worth noting what thoughts come to mind. Take Star of Bethlehem (for shock and trauma) for instance. If you take it, you might find an unrelated thought suddenly pop into your mind. Very often, this is the key to what is causing your problem, so take note and let it pass through its healing stages.

Holding the Thought

It's a good idea to hold the event that is causing your problem in your mind when taking the remedy. I find this has the effect of clearing the emotional impact much faster.

Breaking the 7 Remedy Limit

General wisdom states that the maximum amount of remedies you can take at one time is seven. Generally they are mixed into one bottle and taken a minimum of four times a day.

If you mix too many together, the vibrations get 'muddied', especially if they don't complement each other's vibrations.

I've found that you can get past this limit by taking the remedies one after the other, rather than all at the same time. I've taken up to 15 at a time, using this method, and achieved the desired results. I tend to wait around 20 seconds between doses.

Categories of the remedies.

Doctor Bach divided the remedies into seven categories. However, over the years, I've concluded that there appear to be two more.

With respect to his work, I would like to add the categories of Exhaustion and Depression.

I feel this makes more sense, as some remedies do not quite fit in with certain categories.

It should be worth noting that the remedies may have more than one use and do not always fit neatly into the chosen category. There are always nuances.

These will be noted as best as I can.

Doctor Bach colour coded each section.

Fear

Uncertainty

Lack of Interest in life

Loneliness

Easily influenced

Despondency or Despair

Worry / controlling others

Exhaustion

Depression

The Remedies (By Alphabetical Order)

There are 38 remedies in total. Below is the official list as provided by the Bach Centre. It must be noted that this list, official as it is, barely scratches the surface and may even cause one to choose an incorrect remedy. I will expand greatly in the following pages on each remedy.

Affirmations are also suggested for when taking the remedies. You can use your own or the ones at the end of each section.

Agrimony - mental torture behind a cheerful face
Aspen - fear of unknown things
Beech - intolerance
Centaury - the inability to say 'no'
Cerato - lack of trust in one's own decisions
Cherry Plum - fear of the mind giving way
Chestnut Bud - failure to learn from mistakes
Chicory - selfish, possessive love
Clematis - dreaming of the future without working in the present
Crab Apple - the cleansing remedy, also for self-hatred
Elm - overwhelmed by responsibility
Gentian - discouragement after a setback
Gorse - hopelessness and despair
Heather - self-centredness and self-concern
Holly - hatred, envy and jealousy
Honeysuckle - living in the past
Hornbeam - tiredness at the thought of doing something
Impatiens - impatience
Larch - lack of confidence

Mimulus - fear of known things
Mustard - deep gloom for no reason
Oak - the plodder who keeps going past the point of exhaustion
Olive - exhaustion following mental or physical effort
Pine - guilt
Red Chestnut - over-concern for the welfare of loved ones
Rock Rose - terror and fright
Rock Water - self-denial, rigidity, and self-repression
Scleranthus - inability to choose between alternatives
Star of Bethlehem - shock
Sweet Chestnut - Extreme mental anguish, when everything has been tried and there is no light left
Vervain - over-enthusiasm
Vine - dominance and inflexibility
Walnut - protection from change and unwanted influences
Water Violet - pride and aloofness
White Chestnut - unwanted thoughts and mental arguments
Wild Oat - uncertainty over one's direction in life
Wild Rose - drifting, resignation, apathy
Willow - self-pity and resentment
Rescue Remedy
Rescue Cream

1. Agrimony

Symptoms: Presenting a brave face while feeling tortured by inner thoughts. Cheerful on the outside while tormented on the inside.

Category: Loneliness / Depression

Being an empath isn't easy. The fact is that many empaths feel quite miserable within but don't wish to bother anyone with their problems. They will feel tortured or unhappy within, but they may not understand why, that it's not their fault, or that it's not even a normal state to be in.

As a result, they will often ignore those feelings and try to present a brave face to the world. If someone were to ask them, "how are you today", they'll put on a smile and say, "I'm fine."

One of the reasons they will do this is partly because they do not wish to be a bother to people, but they also sense intuitively that others aren't really interested in how they are feeling. Or worse, they will try to fix them up with suggestions.

Nothing is more frustrating to someone than being told to 'get over' something or that their feelings are not valid. It's reasonable to say that sometimes you don't want someone to solve your "problems"; it's enough to be able to just say what you feel and be accepted or validated.

Another reason why Agrimony Empaths hold their feelings within is that they feel it's a sign of weakness or failure by feeling like they do.

To the Agrimony Empath, this state of being is like a living hell. There is no reason they can understand as to why they would feel this way, and there is no light at the end of the tunnel that things will get better.

Seasonal energies can enhance the feelings. Each season has its own energy. Autumn or Fall, while things are dying and going to seed, can be a particularly depressing time. Spring can often bring new hope and make the empath feel wonderful, even for a short while, as the renewing energies abound.

Denying your feelings and trying to act as though all is fine is not a healthy state to be in, both mentally and physically. It can often lead to psychological disorders, great rage and anger. Also, dis-ease and illness can result.

The Agrimony remedy can help in easing the feeling of needing to hide all those feelings within. While it resolves the happy façade, it's one step in a series of steps to help stop the torturous feelings.

> *It's worth mentioning that the Agrimony Empath often feels much fear and anxiety. This kind of anxiety, while being picked up from others or energies that are out there, can also be caused by the lack of trust in the process.*
>
> *By this I mean they don't trust that all will be well. In fact, the very belief that everything will turn out fine would go a long way to helping resolve the Agrimony state.*
>
> *There are several remedies that will aid here. They are Aspen, Gentian and Gorse. Also Impatiens is powerful because often in the Agrimony state, there is a fear that things aren't happening fast enough.*
>
> *Willow will also help (as that deals with victim / poor me dramas) and Pine (as that deals with the guilt of bothering others.)*

Affirmations:

- I no longer need to hide my feelings from others.
- I have as much right to express myself as others.

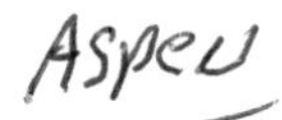

2. Aspen

Symptoms: Vague feelings of discomfort. Unknown fears. Feelings of impending doom. Butterflies in the stomach. Anxiety.

Category: Fear

Aspen is an amazing remedy for the empath. Personally, I believe that everyone should be carrying a bottle around with them.

Every empath, at some point, will suddenly feel terrible for no reason that they can fathom. Things might be going along nicely, when all of a sudden they get that sinking feeling in the pit of their stomach. They get panicky and feel sure that something is wrong, but they can't work out exactly what.

It's very hard for the Aspen Empath to explain to others why they feel this way. Most non-empaths will not understand and will look at you blankly, wondering what you are talking about.

Feelings like vague fears, the sense that something isn't quite right, that something terrible is going to happen, or that something is wrong are very common.

What is actually going on is that we're picking up messages, but they are not coming through clearly. You are only getting vague impressions or half the information. You feel that something is going on with someone or something, but you can't place how and why.

As mentioned, this can also lead to an Agrimony state, especially as the empath seems to have little or no control over these feelings.

Aspen will bring amazing relief to such feelings. The butterflies of anxiety will settle down, and you will know that all will be fine.

Aspen can also help protect against negative astral influences and protect against nightmares or disturbed sleep.

Sometimes taking Aspen may help clarify what the fear is, so you will know what you are afraid of. If this does not stop the fear, then the state moves into known fears. For that the remedy would be Mimulus.

> *It is true that anxiety is the mainstay of many empaths. Many people choose to go to a doctor to see if they can get help, and are often prescribed anti-depressants,*

which can end up doing more harm than good.

When an empath feels such anxieties, there are often unresolved fears at the base of it, and by unresolved, I mean that they have situations that they have not looked at yet or faced. The fears may stem from anything, such as something you will need to do in the future where the outcome is still in doubt, or something you should have done, but put off for example.

While it is true that it will also stem from astral influences, the anxiety is generally due to something that is resonating with the empaths themselves. Aspen does have the ability to not only help reassure and clarify, but to bring such fears into perspective.

Other remedies that will assist with the Aspen state are Gentian, Cerato, and Wild Oats. The last two are for helping to clarify what is bothering you, and showing you which direction to take.

If you are using it to stop nightmares or night terrors, Mimulus and Walnut compliment it well.

> *On that subject, never go to sleep while meditating, or mind travelling. Always bring yourself out of those states and ensure any chakras you have opened are returned to a normal level, otherwise you may be vulnerable to a very unpleasant sleep period.*

Affirmations:

- Whatever is bothering me will become clear to me.
- My anxiety levels are dropping.

3. Beech

Symptoms: Critical of others. Pot calling the kettle black syndrome. For those who are judgemental.

Category: Controlling others

I thought a lot about the remedy Beech. How it fits into being an empath. At first glance, I wasn't sure that it did, but thinking more on it, I think many empaths could actually use Beech.

Beech types are critical of others. They may be intolerant of others' lifestyles, behaviours, beliefs, failings, etc. They will feel irritable when people don't live up to their expectations. They do not suffer fools gladly.

It's with some interest that I note this because I was discussing the suffering fools gladly thing only a few weeks ago with my guides. They asked, 'what is a fool, anyway?', and if a fool has come into your life, maybe it's a chance to demonstrate who you are and show understanding and compassion. If one feels another is a fool, and judges them by their own criteria, then maybe it is they who are the fool.

> *To actually call someone a fool is to make a judgement on their soul agenda, which you*

> *would not likely be privy to. While it is true that people do what we consider to be a lot of foolish actions, or say what we consider foolish things, it also should be considered as to why they have come into your lives. Perhaps they are different perspectives? Perhaps they are demonstrations on what not to do. Perhaps they are an opportunity for you to show tolerance and help bring out the best in others. Whatever the reason, they are not randomly in your life.*

The empath may be aware of much more information that many less empathic people are. Some things are wide open to them and appear so obvious that they can't understand how others can't possibly see it. In fact, sometimes it's so obvious that they will assume that people have seen it and have decided that they do not wish to act upon it.

To them, it's like seeing toast burning and no one reacting, and you just assume, well, maybe they just like their toast burnt.

So the empath can see what appears to be in plain sight. And this can be frustrating to them as they cannot understand why others do not see this. They may consider slow action or the lack of it a waste of valuable time, especially if they have to go over the same things again.

This is also connected to the Impatiens state. We become impatient with others because they do not respond to what we believe they should. Often it's due to a fear that it will reflect badly on ourselves and impact our reputation, or that the blame for others' failures will fall to us. This is common if you are in a manager position at work.

> *It is reasonable to say that the fear is founded, as people are always looking for someone else to blame. By focusing their attentions on another, they focus it away from themselves. This is a common technique for those who are doing something they do not wish others to be aware of, so they accuse others of the same things. In fact, all it does is eventually draw attention back to the person making the accusation.*
>
> *This is also a form of attack. If you want to bring someone down, you focus on the negatives and ignore the good things they do. It's actually a very destructive way to live, but entire societies are based on that premise. Just look at political systems.*

The Beech Empath may experience these feelings of anger and frustration a lot, and may be prone to outbursts of irritability about the people or things not working.

As mentioned, it's also not unusual for the Beech type to be critical of the very same things they, themselves, are guilty of.

It may also be an energy that you had picked up during your childhood and growing up where others were always being very critical of you, and you may now be over sensitive to critical people.

The Bach Flower Remedy Beech brings relief from those feelings. Compassion and understanding replaces feelings of irritability and frustration.

This is also useful for those who love to or feel the need to judge others. Many are forever judging, rarely caring if they are right or not. Entire careers are based on this, especially in today's socially connected world.

Enormous harm can be done because of this and the empath is just as guilty as non-empaths.

Other remedies that compliment Beech are Impatiens and Holly. Also Willow is useful for when one feels they are being a victim themselves, and is unable to see the other person's point of view.

Affirmations:

- I am tolerant of other people's choices.
- Everything has its place.

4. Centaury

Symptoms: Being unable to say no. Being used as a doormat. Putting others interest ahead of your own.

Category: Easily influenced

Being an empath has its own set of problems. Many see themselves as part of something greater, and what affects one affects everyone. They will often put others interests ahead of their own. They would rather go without and make sure everyone else is happy before looking after themselves.

Sadly, many people take advantage of these people and what should be treated with respect gets abused quite badly.

There are people who will ask more and more from a person, never stopping to think they are overloading them, or even caring if they do.

And there are those who will do whatever is asked of them, regardless if they can handle it or not.

This is the Centaury Empath, the person who can't say 'no' to others. Their willingness to please and help out inadvertently turns them into a doormat.

The Centaury Empath will often get angry, annoyed, and frustrated at being taken advantage of, but they will continue to do what is asked of them in spite of this.

They will also feel guilty if they indicate that they are already overburdened, or feel that they won't be believed, and that they are just making excuses.

When they do say that they really can't help right now, the one asking the favour will often act as though they are put out, and that it will be a tremendous inconvenience for them to do the task themselves. The Centaury Empath will relent and say, "alright, I'll do what I can", and they then go and do it.

The Centaury Empath can be easily manipulated by those who are less scrupulous.

The Centaury Empath should be a blessing to those around them. They are the movers, the ones who can get things done, the ones who you can go to for help and answers. They are not others personal slaves.

The Bach Flower Remedy – Centaury brings a clearer perspective. It allows the empath to say "no, I can't do this at this time", and not feel guilty or bad about doing so. This remedy helps protect against being dominated and abused, and helps restore the perspective of self-worth.

> *It's worth mentioning that the Centaury type personality also is generally a victim type mentality, too. They hope, in the process of being used and overwhelmed, that someone will actually notice this, and do something about it.*
>
> *This is rarely the case. In this world, it's the squeaky wheel that gets the grease. If you are doing everything that should be done, and more, and things are running smoothly, no one is going to notice.*
>
> *The important thing here is that boundaries are set and stuck to. If others breach them, they should know they have done so. There is no gain, unless you are striving to increase your endurance, or something similar, for taking on the tasks of all and sundry.*

When you eventually move on, they will not notice or understand what you have done for them.

The remedies that compliment Centaury are Holly, Olive, Elm, Oak, Pine and Willow. These remedies help deal with the effects that arise from such abuse.

Affirmations:

- I have as much right to help and assistance as others.
- I do not have an obligation to do everything.
- If people don't like me saying 'no', that's their problem, not mine.

5. Cerato

Symptoms: Lack of confidence in one's feelings. always questioning. seeking answers from others.

Category: Uncertainty

The Bach Flower Remedy, Cerato, is an amazing remedy for those who are always seeking answers.

Empath or not, most of us seek answers, at one time or another, from an outside source. We do not trust what we are feeling and will ask others, sometimes repeatedly, for their views on a choice we need to make.

The Cerato Empath type has even more difficulty trying to work out what they should or should not do because they are picking up information from all around them. They not only pickup on what others are feeling, but often they also pick up the thoughts as well.

It doesn't take much to discourage an empath, especially when they aren't sure of something to begin with. They can easily let another influence what they feel is the right choice for themselves.

As a general rule, the one who doubts their own feelings is always feeling a sense of anxiety, because they not only don't want to trust in what they feel, but they don't want to it to be true either.

Cerato is indeed the remedy for intuition, and it's very potent and useful. Here's the trap, though. People, in general, want something to be a certain way. They check their feelings, and if their feelings don't agree with how they want things to be, they ignore it. They then seek an outside source to help validate what they really want to hear.

They will keep on asking over and over until finally, something, somewhere, will tell them the answer they seek. Once they have that, they will follow that answer, and unless it agrees with their own intuition, it will rarely work out as planned.

Now, this is important, because when you take the remedy, you will get clarity on what your question is, but you still need to trust it. There is little point in asking, if you ignore the answer.

Making something so in your mind does not necessarily mean it is so in your reality.

For instance, say you wish to ask out someone on a romantic date. You are feeling that it's not a good idea, and that it won't work out, but you ignore this anyway, and still ask.

The candidate either says no, or says yes and then changes their mind at the last moment, or worse, the date leads to things that end up being completely undesirable for you. (And possibly the partner.)

Trusting in your intuition and the answer you would have felt when taking Cerato would have saved you a lot of anguish and torment.

You may feel this person is well worth pursuing, and that may be true, but maybe the timing isn't right. Perhaps you need to do something first, or they need to experience something else before they can be with you.

Trusting in your feelings and knowing when to act is key to a successful life.

> *This is one example, but it can be applied to everything else. Just because you don't like the answer, it doesn't mean that it's wrong. But you will, if you listen to your feelings, know which way to go in order to achieve your goal in the end.*

Cerato strengthens intuition. If you are in doubt about a particular course of action, unsure what you should do, and always seeking assistance from anywhere but within, taking this remedy will make it all crystallize.

Remember, feelings are the language of the soul. They are your truth. They can also be confused with what your thoughts and previous experiences are telling you. Indeed, thoughts can feel like feelings, but make no mistake; they are not the same thing.

Your intuition is your road map, your waypoint, your radar, and the GPS of the soul. If you can trust it and follow it, you will never make a mistake. (Though sometimes you might think you have, however it's often in retrospect that you will understand that it wasn't.)

If you need to make a decision, any decision, and you feel uneasy, unsure, anxious, and are constantly seeking reassurance, then Cerato will certainly help. You will know what needs to be done and proceed with confidence.

> *Cerato works well with Wild Oats, Chestnut Bud, and Gentian. These remedies help give the confidence to follow the answers you receive.*

Affirmations:

- I have the answers I seek.
- I trust in what I feel.
- My feelings are my own and no one may tell me I'm wrong.

6. Cherry Plum

Symptoms: Fear of letting go of ones emotions. Feelings of rage and repressed violence.

Category: Fear

Though this will not apply to all empaths, the good majority of them are on a spiritual path. They have set their own rules, ethics, and moral code and will do their best to abide by them. As they progress, they convince themselves that showing anger, being themselves, or revealing their quirkier side, isn't what they should do. So they try and repress it.

This type of conditioning may be due to childhood repression or spiritual ideas picked up from their religion or studies into philosophies.

The person may eventually feel like they are about to burst with anxiety and grief, but they just can't let go and thus head into a nervous breakdown.

So is born the Cherry Plum type personality: out there on some levels and yet repressed on others. The Cherry Plum Empath has repressed their feelings on certain subjects for so long that they fear what would happen if they choose to let it go and express them.

They may work themselves into a state of frustration that can often take place when they are alone.

Perhaps they may feel cynical and have sardonic thoughts about things that they consider important, or maybe they feel violent tendencies that would shock all around them that think they know the person.

The frustration is often when they do feel they know the answers, but others are running around with seemingly inane ideas or lack of insight, especially on subjects or events that they feel are going to make a difference to them or the world.

But the Cherry Plum Empath does not wish to offend and does not wish to impose their views on others. They are already disillusioned that no one will listen to them anyway. In fact, when someone does come up with the answer, it will be one they have already suggested, but no one took any notice of. Hence the frustration and anger builds.

The Cherry Plum Empath may often catch themselves thinking violent thoughts. They may find themselves imagining throwing a knife at somebody, or perhaps blowing something up.

Not that this empath is violent. It's the opposite. It is repressed frustration that leads to anger, which leads to rage, which will eventually lead to an explosion and health problems.

Cherry Plum is the remedy for this type of empath. It will help allow the person to express who they are without fear.

They will find themselves acting freely and doing and saying things they would have thought they couldn't do, and they will feel good about it.

Others around them will also see the change and react to it. More often than not, the reaction will be positive as they see the person being more who they really are, and not something that they believe they should be.

Cherry Plum is one of the five remedies in the Rescue Remedy.

> *The Cherry Plum type is also very volatile. You might liken it to a pressure cooker that lets off steam every so often, but the majority of the pressure is still contained*

within. If the steam has no outlet, there's a risk that it will eventually explode, with quite devastating results.

Fear is at the base of this emotion. It's the fear of being rejected, and the fear that the reputation that you've spent so much time creating will be shattered if you do anything out of character.

It is true that people tend to judge harshly, especially when they are coming from a place of fear themselves.

Many a repressed child will become a Cherry Plum type, and they will have been taught, normally by their parents or peers that it's not okay to express who you are.

Cherry Plum is the steam escape valve that allows the pressure to dissipate.

Other remedies that work well with this one are Rock Water, Mimulus and Holly.

Affirmations:

- I am allowed to express my feelings to others.
- I am able to let go of my frustration and anger.
- It's okay to be me.

7. Chestnut Bud

Symptoms: Failure to learn from past mistakes. Repeating errors without learning from them.

Category: Lack of Interest in life

As an empath, one of your driving forces may be to help others and make the world a better place. Someone may be in trouble and you, the empath, will do the best you can to help them.

But some of us are drawn to those who thrive on negative energies and control dramas. It doesn't matter what you do for this type of person, the moment you've helped them resolve their issues, they will always move to a new drama.

I'm sure we've all known people like that. They are draining, clingy, demanding of your attention and get angry if you decide that enough is enough, and you will no longer give them your focus.

The empath's natural response to those in need is that their heart goes out to them. They will help them time and time again. However, nothing ever changes, and in the end all that ends up happening is that the empath feels used, abused, and angry. They start feeling and acting in ways that they do not wish to, such as bitching about someone behind their back or having feelings of resentment. They feel that they are no longer the person they wish to be.

And yet, they will repeat the same patterns, maybe with another person, time and time again for perhaps all their life.

Such is the way of the Chestnut Bud Empath. They will repeat the same mistakes over and over again. They do not appear to learn from their past experiences and break out of the cycle they have found themselves in. All the warning signs may be there, but they are not heeded nor understood.

Of course, repeating the same mistake over and over isn't limited to just helping the wrong type of person; it could be anything, such as maybe choosing the wrong partner again and again, or confiding in the wrong type of person, or making the wrong type of purchase. The list can go on.

Chestnut Bud is the remedy that helps stop patterns from being repeated. Those who take it become aware of their decisions, and how it will impact them. They will become more discerning about whom they help, what they do, and how they will act and react.

> *This type of person often has an ego investment when helping others or making decisions about things. What tends to happen is that they have their version of*

how things should be, but it doesn't marry up with how things really are at the moment.

They may well see what will happen, but ignore the warning signs because they do not like what they see. They believe that they can overcome the odds and get lucky.

They may get 'lucky', but what generally tends to happen is that they just end up shooting themselves in the foot.

Often, the reason why things do not work out is because it's something the person is doing. They may be stubbornly acting in a manner that produces negative results, or they may ignore important factors such as timing.

Because there's an ego investment in the outcome, the subject will be unwilling to see or admit that they are wrong, even if it hurts themselves in the process. This is most frustrating to those around them because it's never their fault that things fail. They will be a victim of circumstances.

It's interesting that such people are willing to forgo their inner peace just to make a point that no one else will actually care about.

Chestnut Bud will help with the problems of the ego that stops it from making the correct choices.

This is actually interesting, because I've never thought about this being a remedy to help someone with an ego problem.

Many problems are actually caused by an unhealthy ego. You will find that many of the remedies help this. Chestnut Bud is particularly useful for helping the ego because a good majority of the problems are due to people not listening to or taking the advice of those who may know better.

Remember, we should trust our feelings as to what we should do, and we can often get different perspectives from others.

The Chestnut Bud type tends to ignore everything except what they want to hear.

Now, it should be made clear that we're talking about an unhealthy ego here - one that separates and stops you from growing.

Ego is simply your sense of self, and we need it to do what we do in order to experience who we are. It's when we believe we have all the answers and refuse to listen to anyone else that problems occur.

I think we've all been caught doing that from time to time.

A wise person will always check all the fact available first before jumping to conclusions, and even then, they will then trust in what they feel, as sometimes, even with all the facts present, things aren't always what they appear to be.

This remedy works well with Beech, Cerato, and Wild Oats.

Affirmations:

- I am learning from the experiences of the past.
- I will not repeat the same mistakes twice.

8. Chicory

Symptoms: Narcissistic. Overblown ego. Selfish, manipulative, possessive love. Using guilt to control others.

Category: Controlling others

A Chicory type personality is one who uses guilt to control others. If the attention is not on them, they will create a drama in some way in order to redirect it back to them.

This may be in the form of a tantrum, or a poor me / victim scenario, or perhaps they suddenly get sick, developing a migraine or by having an asthma attack.

I also feel that the Chicory state is the 'Narcissist' state, due to the ego involved. Empaths can be narcissists and use their empathy as a tool to hook into others and manipulate them.

This type of empath will often ignore the current conversation and start their own. If someone is already engaged in a chat, they may well ignore that and start speaking to them themselves, thus trying to draw the energy and conversations to them.

> *Generally, the Chicory type personality could also be referred to as an energy*

vampire. While well-meaning for the most part, they always have an agenda whenever they do something for you. Rarely is something ever done unconditionally, and such personalities have been the staple fodder of situation comedies over the years, where the mother is over domineering.

They are very dangerous to the high-level empath, as they can seriously drain their energies and hamper their growth.

Yes, because the empath is vulnerable to feelings, and because some come with an overwhelming desire to serve and please, it makes them very vulnerable to such people.

That is especially true of family members, because, as a general rule, the vibrational energy of the family resonates with all members, so what affects one, normally affects the others.

If an empath is a Chicory type of personality, they can more easily hook into how someone is feeling, and often use that information to gain the attention they seek. The frustrating part of dealing with a Chicory type is that if you are having a bad day, you can't tell them, because they will make it all about them.

This is also something that helps foster the Cherry Plum state of being. The target learns to keep all their emotions tightly within, in case they are used against them, as a Chicory type will use what you say, even if it's in confidence, against you when it suits them.

This not only is frustrating but can also eventually cause anger and even rage over a long period of time, as the sense of injustice is felt, even many years later.

The Chicory type has learned this type of behavior because of their own conditioning. They weren't able to gain energy in a healthy way, so they had to resort to other methods to do so.

This makes them as much a victim of their own devices as their target, because they are stuck in a perpetual drama, which leaves them desperately empty and unhappy.

The Bach Flower Remedy, Chicory, is very helpful for such people, as it helps to resolve the fear of being alone, and the person will be able to give unconditionally and gain positive energies from that simple action.

My own experiences are that with a Chicory type personality, if they are suffering, they would prefer that everyone else suffer along with them.

This is so, but as a rule, few people are willing to join in their suffering. It is not unusual, though, for people to do what they feel is needed in order to keep the peace, but this is a short to medium term solution to the problem at best.

There is no joy in being in the Chicory state. The hardest thing for the person is to admit they are doing this in the first place. Once again, there is an ego investment in place, and it's only when they've gone as low as they can go and have lost all they consider dear to them, that they start to reassess that maybe they need to change something within.

Indulging a Chicory type is neither healthy for them nor you. You just end up reinforcing their behavior.

It is useful, when they are not in this state, to make them aware of what they are doing and give suggestions as to what they can do to avoid it.

Complimentary remedies to help deal with a Chicory type include Pine, Heather Centaury, and Walnut.

Affirmations:

- I do not need to always be in the right.
- I accept that it's okay to be wrong. It's how I grow.
- I am loved and do not need others to prove it to me.

Clematis

9. Clematis

Symptoms: Dreamy. ungrounded. Helps brings one back to consciousness. Dizziness.

Category: Lack of Interest in life

This is a good remedy for those who have fainted, feel light-headed or dizzy or who can't seem to bring them focus back to a 3D level.

For the empath, it's not unusual for such people to want to be anywhere but 'here' because 'here' may not feel a very nice place to be.

The empath will often try to escape their body, often entering into a dream or fantasy world, having incredible adventures in other parts of the universe or other dimensions. Some create sagas that may go on for years.

The natural inclination for the Clematis Empath is to leave their body, as soon as they feel uncomfortable. This makes them ungrounded and unable to cope with crowds, bad situations, traumatic events, etc.

Being ungrounded is one of the things any empath should ideally avoid as it can have a negative effect on their long-term health.

Clematis is the remedy for grounding. It will help bring the spirit back into the body, and help keep you focused and here.

It is important to note, though, that while Clematis will help you ground, you still need to look at the causes for becoming ungrounded in the first place.

> *The Clematis type personality tends to also work on several levels at the same time, and contrary to what you have stated, it is actually possible to be 'out there' and grounded at the same time.*

Isn't that a contradiction in terms?

> *It's a dichotomy, but it's still possible. Just because you are mind travelling, it does not mean you are ungrounded. The Clematis state is for one who is not only mind travelling, but unaware of their physical surroundings. By this I mean, they may appear dreamy, vague, or they may even be unconscious.*

So, how does one be grounded and ungrounded at the same time?

> *I didn't say that they were ungrounded. I said that they were working on several levels at the same time. This means that the person might be very grounded but*

Clematis

also mind travelling. It's a skill that does take some practice, but essentially, it's multi-tasking.

Okay, then. So, any suggestions for the Clematis type?

As was discussed in the section on being ungrounded, self-confidence is often a key to being grounded. While Clematis helps bring back the person to their body, other remedies should also be considered.

Important ones are Larch, Star of Bethlehem, and Honeysuckle.

Finally, Clematis is one of the five remedies in the Rescue Remedy ™.

Affirmations:

- I am grounded.
- I enjoy being here.

10. Crab Apple

Symptoms: Need for perfection. feelings of being unclean. cleansing. Feeling violated. Self-loathing. Obsessive compulsive disorder.

Category: Despondency or Despair / Fear

The empath picks up a lot of, what I tend to call, psychic pollution. That is negative energies that we tend to absorb like a sponge.

Sometimes it can feel like you've got a dark layer of sewage clinging to your aura.

It's not unusual for the empath to feel polluted or violated by another's aura or energy. This may happen in crowds, parties, or places where the vibrations are negative or low. The empath's first response will be to get away from such areas and people as soon as it's politely possible.

While there are many ways of helping to cleanse your energies, such as showers, smudging, meditation, etc., the Bach Flower Remedy Crab Apple is able to help with those feelings of being polluted or unclean.

If you're anything like me, you will hate feeling unclean, sticky, or grubby. I'm one of those types who need a shower once a day or I won't be able to sleep or feel comfortable until I do.

Crap Apple is the cleansing remedy. It should be taken when one feels violated, or an act has taken place that makes them feel less than savory. This can also apply to sexual activity, too.

The other benefit to this remedy is for those empaths who are perfectionists. Whenever they have done something, they also think they could have done it better.

Taking this remedy will help the user feel less polluted and less critical of their achievements.

> *The Crab Apple type has a lot of trouble feeling comfortable in their body. Natural bodily functions tend to repel them, and often the very thought of being human makes them feel squeamish.*
>
> *Those who are germaphobes, that is, those who are afraid of germs, or have an obsessive-compulsive disorder where they need to be keep washing themselves will benefit greatly from this remedy.*
>
> *The Crab Apple type often has a fear that they will be hurt by germs or anything unsanitary. This could be due to upbringing, or even be past life related, as there are many people who have gotten very sick and passed on through living in unsanitary conditions.*

> *Sixteen drops of Crap Apple in a bath is a very good cleanser for the body. It helps the physical and also cleanses the energies.*
>
> *It's also a good idea to put a few drops into a spray bottle and spray it into areas that feel heavy or polluted with negative energies.*
>
> *As mentioned, Crab Apple does have the ability to make one less of a perfectionist. An empath who is on their spiritual path may never be happy with what they are doing. Even if they achieve amazing results, they never give themselves credit or feel that their work is worth releasing to the world.*
>
> *It works very well with Rock Water, Star of Bethlehem, and Sweet Chestnut.*

Crab Apple is one of the six remedies of the Rescue Cream ™ and what I believe is the key to what makes the Rescue Cream so effective.

Affirmations:

- I feel clean and wholesome.
- My work is good and worth letting others see.
- It's okay to not have everything perfect.
- Everything is as it should be.

11. Elm

Symptoms: Overwhelmed by too many things.

Category: Exhaustion

The Elm type person is one who has too many things going on at the same time, and they find themselves being overwhelmed.

This normally happens in day-to-day life situations, such as work or too many responsibilities at home.

The empath has another level to consider - being overwhelmed by many feelings at the same time. This may happen in crowds or parties, or even with world events such as elections, disasters, or incidences where emotions run high. It's made even worse when you have several friends who are all going through a bad time.

Elm is the remedy that helps you cope with all waves of things that threaten to overwhelm you. Taking Elm will help you cope with the stress, the feeling of panic, and the belief that you can't cope. It will aid you in calming and centering your emotions and thoughts, and in getting through the busy times where too much is really going on.

As a general rule, no one will take on more than they can actually handle. Still, there is the illusion that you can't handle it all.

Elm assists in not only resolving that belief that you won't cope, but aid you in coping by taking things in the priority that they need to be taken and with the knowledge that all will be well.

The Elm type stems from the fear that if everything isn't done, there will be consequences; and they will be unpleasant ones.

While this may be the case in some situations, it is often not so, and more often than not, things appear to be worse than they seem.

Some people even just throw their hands in the air and walk away. This certainly does not make things any better. Elm will help those who feel they can't cope.

For the empath, it will also help sort and settle the feelings they get when there are too many of them to sort through and understand at the same time.

Useful remedies that work with Elm are Gentian, Larch, Olive, and Oak.

Affirmations:

- I am coping with what is happening.
- I no longer feel overwhelmed.

12. Gentian

Symptoms: Lack of faith. Easily discouraged by setbacks.

Category: Uncertainty / Despondency or Despair

Gentian is an amazing remedy. As empaths, we will often feel discouraged when things go wrong or when our view of the world isn't shared by others.

The empath sees what they consider to be in plain sight. They feel what is going on and can see the probable outcome if the current path is followed. And yet, they appear to be the only one who can see this. In the end, the empath will begin to doubt themselves and their judgment, letting themselves become overwhelmed with the thoughts or beliefs of those around them.

The empath may well think: well, if others can't see this, then maybe it is me who is wrong. Maybe I've missed something that everyone else is seeing.

A feeling of despair and hopelessness flows over them and they stop believing in what appears to be obvious. This feeling can be quite devastating, often stopping a person in their tracks. They start to feel: maybe I'm making this all up, and I'm really deluding myself.

Gentian is the remedy for those who stop believing in what they know and feel to be true, when they feel that things aren't going to work out, and that they aren't going to succeed.

It is the remedy for those who are discouraged by even minor setbacks. If something doesn't flow as they were hoping, they doubt themselves and think: well, maybe no one really wants this, and I'm just bothering others or making a fool of myself.

Gentian should be considered whenever you are doubting your own truths. It's also a useful remedy to take if you don't believe in Bach Flower Remedies!

> *Generally, Gentian types work on theories and the faith that it will all work out in the end. If no one sees what they see, then they tend to assume they were wrong.*
>
> *This is one of the remedy for self-confidence, and as has previously been discussed, being self-confident is important for being grounded.*
>
> *When you believe in yourself and in what you are doing, many things will shift. You will not only find that you start to make progress, but others around you will start to believe in you, too.*

When one has self-doubts, others will pick up on it, and even if you know something is correct, others will tend not to listen because they can see that you don't quite believe it.

People need their advocators to be decisive, firm, and strong in what they are saying. Hedging your bets or putting in qualifiers only serves to create a situation where no one is really confident.

Whatever you do, do it with conviction, even if you do end up being wrong. It doesn't matter if you are in the end, as long as you've recognized it and used the information for the next time you try again.

Failing is just as important as success, for it gives you valuable information, and you've not really failed until you've given up.

As mentioned, this is a good remedy to take when you don't believe that the Bach Flower Remedies actually work.

The other thing to note is that Gentian is the remedy for those easily discouraged by minor setback, but it is not the remedy for those who fall into depression because of minor setbacks. That remedy would be Star of Bethlehem. Also, Cerato and Wild Oats compliment Gentian.

Affirmations:

- Everything will work out fine.
- Even if others can't see what I see, it doesn't mean I am wrong.
- I have faith in my own path.

13. Gorse

Symptoms: Feelings of hopelessness and despair. Seeing no point in continue to go on or live.

Category: Despondency or Despair

Gorse is the remedy for when you feel there is no hope left. You are at the end of your tether. You have tried everything, and you no longer see any point to trying.

This differs from the Sweet Chestnut state where you need to embrace a new belief system in order to move on.

This is useful when someone sees no point in going on, especially after something like a traumatic death. They may be quietly suicidal and are ready to so something such as step in front of an oncoming train.

> *Gorse should be taken by empaths that have had a long history of being misunderstood and are unable to fit in. They normally have tried what they believe to be everything, but this is not the case, as there are solutions to every problem.*
>
> *The thing about the empath who is in the Gorse state is that they no longer hold any hope for themselves. They may try*

something just to please another, but they don't believe that it will work.

This comes normally after a series of failures that they are unable to fathom the reasons for.

Taking Gorse restores hope and returns optimism. It's also very useful for dealing with depression caused by perpetual failure.

Gorse works well with Gentian, Sweet Chestnut, Star of Bethlehem, and Willow.

Affirmations:

- Things will get better.
- I am feeling optimistic.
- Things are not as bad as I believe them to be.

14. Heather

Symptoms: Fear of being alone. Loneliness.

Category: Loneliness

The Heather personality type is one who is afraid of being lonely. They may not like their own company and fear being alone.

Their main trait is that they talk excessively. So much so, that it's difficult to get a word in edgeways, and often they will talk at you rather to you.

Generally, people avoid the Heather personality type as they tend to tell you their life story, and that of their parents, cousins, friends, and acquaintances with mind numbing details.

The empath will find this type of interaction an incredible drain on their energies, both mental and spiritually.

Many empaths are good listeners, and because they wish to help others, they can easily become trapped by the Heather type.

> *Generally, when one is a Heather type, it's due to them fearing their own company. There are empaths who feel very afraid,*

lonely, and vulnerable and do not like who they are.

Other people tend to have a stabilizing effect on such empaths. It's not unusual for their feelings of frustration, anger, or violent feelings to completely vanish the moment they are with someone else, especially if it's a friend.

The Heather personality type is always in some sort of drama, and their problems are always very important. But to the listener, it's mostly humdrum and tedious to listen to.

By talking, it's the way that they get energy from others, as they have cut themselves off from their own source. This makes them dangerous to empaths, and if the empath is a Heather type them self, they are in danger of being codependent; that is, relying on others to feel good about themselves.

It should be noted that not all Heather types fear their own company. Often it's the fear of ending up alone. This remedy may be useful when a relationship is on the verge of a break up and you are hanging on because you fear the loss of companionship.

This type of Heather state does not necessarily mean that you seek attention, talk excessively, or even seek out company. It may manifest as a quiet loneliness and isolated life.

> *Heather helps with the fear of loneliness and low self-esteem. It works well with Larch, Mimulus, Water Violet and Willow.*

Affirmations:

- I no longer feel lonely.
- I have all the friends and companionship I need.
- I do not mind my own company.

15. Holly

Symptoms: anger. jealousy. envy. hatred. distrust

Category: Fear

There are certain remedies that come up time and time again for empaths. Holly is one of them.

While the remedy is good for jealousy, envy, hate and distrust, the main emotion that many empaths feel is anger.

They perceive so much injustice, and they often feel impotent to be able to do anything about it.

Anger is a big problem for the empath who is on the spiritual path. For some reason, they believe that they must not get angry. They try to forgive the trespasses against them, but all that happens is that they feel like they are letting others get away with their actions, and that they are allowing themselves to be abused.

The next stage is they try to repress the anger, and then become angry about not being allowed to express anger. This leads to a sharp, psychic type of headache, which tends to center around the third eye area, and can also lead to the Cherry Plum state.

Taking Holly won't make the situation change, but rather your anger will no longer have any control over you. You will experience a shift in perspectives and know that everything is as it should be.

For the empath, it's a remedy that's certainly worth keeping handy.

> *One of the things the empath needs to be aware of is that the anger is often used to trigger and control them into actions that they would not normally otherwise take. If you wish to make someone act out of character, or do something they normally wouldn't do, you make them angry, indignant, or self-righteous.*
>
> *In other words, anger is used by others to push the buttons to make people react in the ways they desire.*
>
> *There are many people and entities that would enjoy seeing someone's spiritual 'fall', that is, act in a perceived unspiritual manner.*
>
> *This is done to either prove a point, for example, that the person who is acting spiritually is not really what he claims to*

be, or to try and reduce the growth and threat of a light-worker.

No one really wins when someone gets angry. It doesn't help anything, except create negative energies. If the anger is not dealt with, it can have long-term repercussions for both parties, as such energies create karmic bonds that can easily transcend this life and spill into other lives or astral levels.

Taking Holly greatly aids the feelings of anger and hostility and injustice that comes up from time to time.

Holly works well with Willow, White Chestnut and Walnut.

Affirmations:

- My anger has no control over me.
- I forgive those who make me angry for they know not what they do.
- I have no need for envy or jealousy as I will always get what I need.
- My feelings are my guide for if I can trust someone.
- I have no need for hate. I am unconditional love.

16. Honeysuckle

Symptoms: Absorbed by the memories of the past. Regrets. Stuck in 'the good old days'. Nostalgia.

Category: Lack of Interest in life / Despondency or Despair

The Honeysuckle type is for those who are absorbed by memories of past times. Sometimes they may be great memories, but they may also be periods that they did not like or enjoy back in the day.

They are often overcome with nostalgia, and view things through rose tinted glasses.

They remember how it used to be, how things were much better, and life was good.

This is another form of escapism. Where the Clematis type is dreamy and is anywhere but here, the Honeysuckle type tries to escape to better times.

I believe that they can also be past unresolved issues, that you go back over time and time again, playing out ''what if's' in your mind.

Honeysuckle is the remedy for letting those memories go and coming back to the here and now.

Honeysuckle types generally are drawn to more pleasurable memories when things are not going well for them. The empath may find this occurring when they are in a situation they wish had never occurred, and the feelings and emotions of those around them are too unpleasant and intense to deal with.

When you are drawn to past memories, you tend to zone out of the present, and you fail to notice what is going on around you.

What can be occurring here is that there is still some unresolved energy that has not been dealt with yet. It could be guilt, unresolved feelings, an embarrassing situation (which more often than not, only you would even remember, let alone care about), or something along those lines.

Honeysuckle aids in resolving those old links and consolidating them so you can move on and focus on what needs to be done in the moment. It also helps resolve past regrets you may have.

The remedies that compliment it depend on what the memories are, but generally, Star of Bethlehem and Pine can prove to be useful here.

Affirmations:

- I let go of the past and the emotions associated with it.
- I am in the here and now and things will be better than ever.
- I resolve all past feelings so I may move forward.

17. Hornbeam

Symptoms: Weariness. Mondayitis. Procrastination.

Category: Exhaustion

Sometimes we feel we don't have the energy to face the day. Everything is too much of an effort, and we'd rather avoid it. This normally happens when we face the same things day in and day out, such as our day job or tedious chores such as household work that we may not take pleasure in. (Though, even if you do enjoy something, you can eventually feel burnt out on it, too.)

We may not feel like we have the energy to do the tasks, but should something different come up, we suddenly find the energy to deal with it.

This is the Hornbeam state of mind. It's what we call, Mondayitis, or boredom. It is brought on by the lack of variety in certain things, and the fact that we don't always get the stimulation that we crave.

We might look at a task and think: I really can't face this right now.

It is also a sign that you've done something too many times. Such as a performance you have to give every night or a having to do a task you didn't enjoy to begin with. It can help with having to sit through things that you consider boring.

Hornbeam gives us the energy to face the day and deal with those things we do not wish to deal with. It removes the feeling of fatigue and weariness.

> *This is an important remedy for empaths as many empaths do find themselves not only drained by their daily routine, but being drained by the same demands from others around them.*
>
> *For those who constantly feel this way, it's worth keeping a bottle of Hornbeam in your pocket.*

What I don't get is why we get so tired so quickly, even if it's with something we want to do.

> *It's mainly because our energy works on several levels, and when one level is cut off, the blockage causes fatigue.*
>
> *There is the physical level, the spiritual level, the emotional level, and the 'chi' level, to name the main ones. Chi is our esoteric*

energy that we draw on from the universe, or if you rather, the stuff of life.

When one level gets depleted, we tend to fall back on other levels, and they become rapidly depleted, too, as we are unable to keep up.

Even a lot of sleep doesn't always help, as we're not dealing with the main issue that is causing the drain. In fact, sleep is often a way of avoiding facing those issues, hoping to try speed your time away.

Hornbeam is one of those remedies that helps replace the links to your energies, specifically the chi.

Affirmations:

- I have the energy I need to do my tasks.
- I have the desire to get things done.
- I find joy in even the most mundane of things.

18. Impatiens

Symptoms: Patience. For those who are quick thinking but impatient. Impulsive. Irritation. Frustration.

Category: Fear / Worry

Impatiens is aptly named because it is the remedy for being impatient. If you are quick thinking, able to see outcomes faster than others, or just in a hurry for things to happen, then Impatiens may be the remedy to take.

Empaths may find this useful as they often find many aspects of their life dreary. For many such empaths, the mental stimulus of small talk just isn't enough for them. They will tap their foot impatiently while enduring the minor details that others are fascinated by.

It is also handy for when someone can't keep up due to old age, Alzheimer's, people who are hard of hearing or those who are no longer capable or as fast as they once were.

It may be useful for those who become frustrated or angry with themselves for making mistakes or not being able to do things fast and perfectly enough.

It's the remedy for patience.

For the empath on the spiritual path, things often just don't move fast enough. They want it all now, and if that means taking short cuts, then they will try and do so.

This is very dangerous in some situations, especially when you're looking at gaining spiritual knowledge and power. Too much, too soon, and you stand a great risk of burning out.

This is especially true for those who are working to raise their Kundalini energy.

And the Kundalini for the initiated is?

It's the force that helps attune you to the greater energies of the universe. It rests at the base chakra, which is at the base of your spine, and as it awakens, it will travel through each chakra, awakening it and the associated powers.

Once it reaches the heart, much caution should be exercised. You then have the throat, third eye, and the crown chakras. The last two are especially dangerous if you are not attuned to the energies. You'd be basically frying your senses, your body, and mind with universal energy.

As a general rule, unless you have a master who knows what they are doing, (they are not that common yet), the Kundalini should be best left to rise in its own time.

This might take many years. When you are ready, you will feel the flow of energy spread up your spine. It may be cool, warm, or hot, but it should never be painful. Painful means you need to back off.

Then the feeling may stop, and it may be weeks, months, or even years before you are ready again, depending on what you are doing and how far you are progressing.

For those students who are eager for the energy to rise, Impatiens will help them wait. Timing is everything, and your spirit knows its timing.

Push too fast and far, and you will end up setting yourself back lifetimes.

The body and your soul aspect needs time to adjust.

Now, it is true that there are those who have raised their Kundalini in past lives, and feel they should be able to do it in this one, and it's fair to say that they certainly have a great advantage there, however the body still needs time to acclimatize.

The best example of this that I heard was by author John Gray. In a lecture that I heard on tape, he spoke of how he went for physical therapy where they used electrical pads to help his condition. (I honestly can't remember the details of it, but it's not important.)

The doctor would put the pads on him, turn it up a notch, and John would feel the electrical impulses for a few minutes before the sensation stopped. Then the doctor would turn it up a notch, and once again there was a period of electrical sensation. Over the period of half an hour, it was taken to the appropriate level, and by that time, there wasn't much feeling.

One day before a session, John was waiting, and he decided to put the pads on himself and turn the knob to full. He got quite the jolt. The lesson was that he needed to take it in stages.

Now he was talking about love making in his lecture, but when I heard it, I thought of the Kundalini.

> *It's a good example. Too much, too quick, and it's not a good result.*
>
> *You have witnessed people rising too quickly, and burning out, leaving them worse off than before they started. It's not a pretty outcome.*

Is there anything else worth mentioning?

> *It's a good remedy for emergencies. If you are waiting for medical assistance, or for something vital to happen, Impatiens will reassure you that things will be okay.*
>
> *Also, many empaths by their nature are quite intelligent. They often do not suffer fools gladly. Impatiens is one of those remedies that assist to give you patience for others perceived shortfalls.*
>
> *It's also a very good remedy for when you feel you are pushed for time. It works well with Beech, Elm, and Holly.*

Impatiens is one of the remedies in the Rescue Remedy ™

Affirmations:

- I have plenty of patience.
- I have plenty of time to get things done.
- I know my timing.

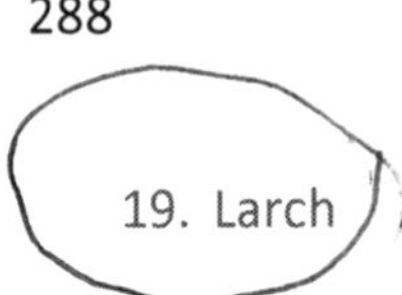

Symptoms: Lack of self-esteem or confidence.

Category: Despondency or Despair / Uncertainty

One of the keys to being grounded is self-confidence. As empaths, many of us suffer not only from low self-esteem, but lack of belief in our convictions.

This often stems from us seeing what others can't see, or feeling what others don't feel, and being the only ones who seem to be perceiving it.

This leads to self-doubts and the feeling of invalidation. The empath often feels that they are just crazy.

This is also a good remedy for those who are in a place where they feel they don't belong or fit in.

> *Generally, the empath is currently living in a reality that is co-created by those who do not believe in the unity of the soul that is oneness, and the fact that all people are actually psychic as a birth right.*
>
> *It is drummed into people by many religions and belief systems that such things do not exist, or if they do, it's due to us trafficking with something evil, such as the devil.*

This certainly does not help us in the self-confidence department as we come to doubt our own evidence and sense of reality.

It is important that we come to trust what we feel because feelings are our compass to what we are doing and which direction we should head in.

Larch is a very good remedy to help with self-esteem.

I think that it is true that when we are put down enough by others, we start to believe it ourselves, even if what they are saying is not true.

Well, the real point here is, even if what they say is true, does that mean that you are a bad person or should be put down because of it? Does it mean that just because you do, or cannot do, what others feel you should do, or not do, that it somehow makes you wrong?

This is the issue many face. They do not conform to what others believe they should be, and so hide and shield themselves from the rest of the world.

This is very typical behavior for the empath. They act as though they have

> *something to be ashamed of and are mortified if someone else discovers their 'terrible secret'.*
>
> *Being an empath is nothing to be ashamed of. It is a natural state of being. It should be celebrated and enjoyed. It's potential to enrich this world and make it into a happier and joyous place is amazing.*

I know that when I was young, not fitting in certainly had a huge effect on me. Apart from being shy and put down, I also was hit by a car while crossing the road, and it resulted in my coordination being destroyed for many years. I was the only kid in the school to get a negative score when trying to kick a football in the fitness tests for Physical Education.

Somehow, this made me an outcast, and I felt like it was my fault I wasn't good at sports.

Larch certainly would have been useful to have had back then.

Larch is the remedy that helps lack of self-confidence. Taking will help you to accept who you are and know that it's okay to be you. It's okay to be different from the others around you. That being different can be a good thing and is the mother of innovation and creation.

Just because something is considered the norm doesn't mean that it's actually normal.

Larch can also be useful when going for a job interview, meeting people for the first time, or just doing something that you don't feel you're capable of doing. It will help you accept yourself and gain confidence.

> *Remedies that compliment Larch are Gentian and Gorse.*

Affirmations:

- It's okay to be me.
- I have as much right to be here as anyone else.
- Others are not better than me. I am just as good.

20. Mimulus

Symptoms: Fear of known things.

Category: Fear

Mimulus is the remedy for known fears. Unlike Aspen, which is the remedy for vague, unknown fears and anxiety, Mimulus helps us deal with fears such as spiders, heights, loneliness, claustrophobia, and so on.

Is it said that those who embrace their fears will overcome them. Remember, what you resist, persists, and what you look at and embrace disappears.

Some fears are so strong that we can't even begin to look at them. Just the very thought of them sends us into a panic mode. The greatest are things like losing your partner, job, home, etc.

I've always loved this quote from the movie Strictly Ballroom: A life lived in fear is a life half lived.

I can say from personal experience that this remedy works amazingly well, especially when it comes to fear of spiders, insects, etc. I no longer give them a second thought when I see them in my space.

Instead, I see it from a different perspective. I know that the odds of them hurting me or bothering me are extremely low and my intuition will let me know if I need to remove them.

> *For the empath, there is the fear of rejection, of being made to look like a fool or a freak, or perhaps having your reputation tarred with stigma. There is also the fear of failure, or worse (for some) the fear of success, that can often lead to what we perceive to be responsibility which we may not be ready to take on.*
>
> *Fear, while having its uses, generally stops us from doing what we are here to do. It stops us from following our intuition and trusting what we know we should be doing.*
>
> *For instance, if you feel the strong pull to pass on a message to someone, but you have no grounds or reason for doing so, other than a sense that compels you to do so, then fear can stop you from passing it on.*
>
> *It may be the fear that we might look stupid, or that we might sound insane, or perhaps we are afraid of how the other person may react, especially if we barely know them.*

Mimulus is very helpful with helping to overcome those types of fears.

You can be sure, that as an empath, you will have times where you are called to do something that you cannot rationalize away.

Also, fear can stop us from progressing on our spiritual path or from moving onto other things when we sense the time is right.

Other remedies that compliment Mimulus are Gentian, Larch, and Cerato.

Affirmations:

- I have no fears.
- Fear no longer has control over me.
- I see my fears from another perspective.

21. Mustard

Symptoms: Deep gloom for no apparent reason. Removing psychic hooks from others from yourself.

Category: Depression

Mustard is the remedy for gloom with no apparent reason or warning. It's like you suddenly are surrounded in a dark cloud, and there is no rational basis for it. You may feel melancholy or have the 'blues', when nothing is actually wrong, but you feel very depressed.

This state can come and go very suddenly.

> *The Mustard state is something all empaths should be aware of. It is generally brought on by minor setbacks and un-cleared shock and trauma, which are more the causes, not the symptoms.*
>
> *What may be occurring here is that the empath may be under attack by negative entities or around an area of dark energy. This could be a person who is in a very negative state, or a house that has had a traumatic history.*

So, to take this to its logical conclusion, Mustard can help protect you against psychic attacks?

It is one of the remedies, yes. It won't stop the attack, but it will help you in not being affected by them. It will help reconnect you to your own source of light, especially if the attack is to try and block you from doing work that involves positive energy and light.

Mustard states are where you are cut off from your own light and source, and there is nothing you feel you can hang onto because all hope appears to have gone.

It's like entering into a dark bubble where nothing can reach you.

I believe that there are areas of dark and negative energy that we all run in to. It could be localized, or it could be formed by a group of people who are going through a bad experience. Graveyards are especially bad for the empath as they will often have the residue of grief hanging around.

While it's true that such places are not empath friendly, the Mustard state is actually more extreme.

It can be quite debilitating and can also strike during the Fall and Wintertime, when the energies tend to withdraw and the nights are longer and days are cooler.

> *It's also worth noting that some entities can attach psychic links to your astral body and drain you. Mustard removes those links safely.*

Generally, it may be just psychic pollution, which are areas of negative energy.

While mustard is a useful remedy for protecting against gloom, the following may also be of help:

- Having a shower. Water has a cleansing effect, and the empath should at least have one shower a day. See the water as light washing away all the negative and psychic pollution clinging to you.
- Smudging your personal area with sage. This is said to help clear the area of negative energies. It's also good for cleansing your aura. Be aware, however, that if spirits are in this space and they were there before you, it's better to try and negotiate with them rather than force them out.
- Putting the Bach Flower Remedy Crab Apple into a water-filled spray bottle and spraying the mist into the air and your aura. As this remedy is the cleansing remedy, it can be quite useful for that purpose.

- Simply sending thoughts of love and joy around you, though this can be difficult if you are feeling totally gloomy.

It certainly can be hard being an empath with all the gloom and psychic pollution around, however Mustard can certainly help.

> *Remedies that work well with Mustard are Star of Bethlehem, Aspen, Gorse and Sweet Chestnut.*

Affirmations:

- I am not affected by negative energies.
- Any negative hooks in my energy are now safely removed.
- I radiate love, joy and light in any dark places.

22. Oak

Symptoms: Pushed past the point of exhaustion. Feeling beyond your emotional, psychic or physical limits. Chronic fatigue syndrome.

Category: Exhaustion

Oak is the remedy for being pushed past your limits.

For instance, if you do something for a long extended period, and if you are past the point of exhaustion, you are pushing yourself past what would be your healthy limits. This may happen at work, or if you're a caretaker, or if you just have not taken a decent holiday for a very long time.

The Oak type will say, "well, it's got to be done," roll up their sleeves, and get on with it.

> *Empaths are very susceptible to the Oak state, as they are often manipulated by others into doing things they really shouldn't have to do.*
>
> *This is an extension of the Centaury state. When someone can't say no and keeps on taking more and more on, they eventually reach an Olive (exhaustion) state and then move into the Oak state.*

> *The empath who wishes to keep the peace feels that they are the only one capable of doing what must be done or feels guilt has been used to manipulate them.*

Being an Oak type myself, I have often pushed myself way beyond my limits, almost to the point of no return. (Holding down a full-time job, not taking leave, and doing what I do after hours ended up taking its toll.)

Oak is one of the remedies that has often brought me back from the edge. It is the remedy for when you are pushed way past your limits of exhaustion and are literally running on empty.

Oak will help bring you gently back, restore your energies, and stop you from breaking.

Remember, though, it is important to take a break. Even Bach Flower Remedies do have their limits, and while they will get you out of trouble, a change in the behavior that is creating the problems in the first place is the key to permanent healing.

The empath in us will often find it hard to resist the calls that drive us on. Even when we try to rest and ignore it, it's like a constant nagging. It's as though someone has tied an invisible string around your waist and keeps on tugging on it, and sometimes there are tugs from all direction.

Remedies that work well with this one are Centaury, Pine, Olive, and Vervain.

Affirmations:

- I am not the only one who can do this job.
- I respect myself enough not to push myself past my limits.
- It's okay to take a break.

23. Olive

Symptoms: Mental, psychic or physical exhaustion.

Category: Exhaustion

Olive is the remedy for exhaustion.

Traditionally, it is said to be for long-term exhaustion, but I've found it works just as well with any type.

Even after a long week's work, it will help remove the fatigue and tiredness you may feel.

For long-term exhaustion, it can be a real lifesaver. While this remedy does not replace the need for sleep or for taking a proper break, it can sustain you for long periods of time when neither may be available.

> *Empaths should be aware that their energies can easily be depleted by others, leading to exhaustion. This is typical for Lightworkers, who tend to respond to everything that comes their way, and who often treat every case as though there were a time limit on getting it done.*
>
> *It's worth noting that nothing is ever so bad that it must be done immediately. There will be emergency cases, but you will*

> *sense the urgency of those. In general, though, you can take a bit more time to respond.*

Sometimes it feels like people are in a bad situation and really need help. It's hard to ignore them.

> *Responding later, rather than immediately is where the problem lies, and often responding at all is an assumption that this is somehow your responsibility rather than others'.*
>
> *You can only do so much, and if you burn yourself out because you have not looked after yourself, then you will be of little use to anyone, especially as it can take a long time to recover and heal.*
>
> *It is very important to give yourself a break or have a day where you dedicate it to yourself, and it should be regular. If you find yourself in a situation where this is not possible, then you should look at your lifestyle and work out why you are putting yourself in this position. Generally, this is due to the Centaury state, and that remedy should be considered being taken, too.*

I guess it's hard when people seem to develop personal attachments to you and feel upset if you don't have the time to focus on them.

> *Unless you're doing it because it's renewing for you, or uplifting, then you may be doing this for the wrong reasons. Being there for someone, just because they are addicted to your energies, is not healthy for either party.*
>
> *For you, it will seriously drain your energies, and for the other party, you are encouraging this connection, which makes them codependent on you. In the end, neither will gain all that much, except maybe resentment and disappointment.*

The other thing to note with Olive is that you need time to build your reserves of energy back up. You can liken it to a rechargeable battery. For it to work at its maximum capacity, it needs to be charged fully over a period of time. Charging it for a few minutes will give it a little energy, but it will only last a very short time.

The exhausted empath is like that. They may start the day with vigor, but soon they run out of energy. Each day becomes a struggle. They end up taking one day at a time, and wondering how much longer they can keep going like this.

The Bach Flower Remedy Olive brings much needed relief. It is the remedy for exhaustion, long-term or short-term. And while it won't replace a proper break, it will help to re-energize and restore your energies.

Exhaustion, long-term or otherwise is a serious problem, and the best solution is to take a break before you end up suffering long-term damage and are no longer able to function.

It is important to note that most people will not recognize or acknowledge that you are in this state.

> *Generally, many people don't particularly care if you are going to get sick due to being pushed too hard, as long as they get what they need. Most will just put their head in the sand and hope it all goes away. It rarely does, and all you end up with is resentment and anger at being used and abused.*
>
> *In the end, only you can really say that enough is enough and walk away. Trust in the universe to look after you and it will. Easier said than done, but nothing is random, and thus, all things are in place when you are ready to move on.*
>
> *Remedies that compliment Olive are Oak, Centaury, Hornbeam, Pine, and Holly.*

Affirmations:

- I am feeling energized.
- I have permission to take downtime as needed.

- I am not a service that is on 24/7.

24. Pine

Symptoms: Guilt. suicidal tendencies.

Category: Fear / Worry / Depression

Pine is the remedy for guilt.

In my opinion, guilt is the great destroyer. It can literally bring your life to a screeching halt. It can immobilize you and make you wish you were not here.

Empaths suffer from guilt issues because they pick up on the feelings of others and hold themselves responsible for them.

One important thing to remember is this: As long as what you have done has been with the highest of intentions, then you cannot control how another will react. The choice is upon them to choose to be positive or negative. If they choose to react badly to your actions, then that is their issue. You cannot control that.

Guilt is debilitating and often used as a key focus of a psychic attack. I've seen people and businesses almost destroyed by guilt.

Many times, we don't even know we are feeling guilty. All we get is this terrible despairing feeling and no way to hide from it.

Guilt can happen for many reasons:

- Something you have done to another.
- Something that another may have done.
- When your expectations are not being met for another. You will feel bad for them and also feel responsible somehow, especially if you feel connected to whatever the desired outcome is.
- Family and friends are wonderful for making you feel guilty. They can make you feel as though you're the terrible villain and have no appreciation for what they do and the sacrifices they have made... and so on. However, this is a power play and a way of controlling you. Unconditional love will accept you for who you are and not seek to make you feel terrible or control you.
- Guilt can come for wanting to do your own thing instead of what others think you should be doing.
- We can feel guilty if we don't feel a certain way. For instance, if someone dies and we don't continue to grieve for them, we can destroy ourselves with guilt, feeling we are a bad person.
- And of course, there are the things we have done 'wrong' that we feel the worst

> about. Remember, though, no one is part of anything that they didn't agree to on some level. Their experience is what they have received from you, and therein lies the gift you have given them.

It's important to note that as empaths, we are very susceptible to guilt. We pick it up all too easily and sometimes never realize that we have. Coming from a place of guilt is coming from a place of fear, and it may not always bring the desired outcome.

The Bach Flower Remedy, Pine, is excellent at dissolving feelings of guilt. Taking it will bring a new perspective and much needed relief. It will feel as though an incredible weight is lifted, and you will be free to do again what you love doing.

I would consider Pine as being one of the most important Bach Flower Remedies.

> *There isn't much more to add in regards to guilt, save that we should always be checking for it. Depending on our conditioning from childhood and beyond, feelings of guilt can often be triggered within us.*
>
> *I would recommend that you never use guilt to get your own way. You will not only*

create a negative karmic bond with the other party, but you also create a reality where the universe will respond to such manipulations.

When you use guilt to manipulate others, you are making a declaration that you can't get what you desire in other ways. As has been pointed out over the ages, the Universe, God, Energy, or whatever you choose to call it, only reinforced your idea of yourself. If you believe this is what you must resort to, then it will agree with you and provide the experiences as such.

Beware of manipulating others. You do not need to do so. Find another way or eventually you risk descending into your own personal version of Hell, though it may take many lives to reach there.

Whatever you choose to do, do it with conviction, but come from a place of love.

Pine works well with Centaury and Walnut.

Affirmations:

- Guilt has no control over me.
- I am not responsible for how other people feel.
- I can't control how others choose to react toward what I do.

25. Red Chestnut

Symptoms: over-concern or fear for the welfare of loved ones. Always worrying about others.

Category: Fear / Worry / Controlling others

Red Chestnut is the remedy for when you are always worrying about other people. These people may not need worrying about, but still the worry is there.

Empathy can be a curse or a blessing, depending on your point of view. It helps you to keep track of your friends and family. You can always 'probe' energetically to make sure all is well.

The Red Chestnut Empath tends to worry too much about others, though. They are always concerned that something bad may happen to a loved one.

The empath is always imagining something bad is going to happen. That they may be in an accident, attacked, meet with bad luck, and so on.

Not only does it put undue pressure on the person they are worrying about (as they will always feel a pull no matter what they are doing), but there is an actual danger of the things that are being worried about manifesting, as that is where the thoughts and energies are directed to. (And enough thought eventually creates and manifests itself.)

Personally, I find it very stressful when people try to help me when I'm going through a rough time, energy-wise. They will insist on talking to and interrogating me to try to find solutions, when all I need is to be left alone, not talk to anyone, and do what I need to do so I can heal myself. Unless someone is specifically asking for help, do not insist on helping them. You are not helping. You are actually making it worse. Sometimes just being there is enough.

Red Chestnut is the remedy that helps with the over-concern for the welfare and safety of others. If you find that are always worrying about someone, this remedy will bring relief.

> *When you worry about another, you have not remembered that all is in perfect order. Nothing happens to us without our permission on some level, and that means that your loved ones are safe, unless they are choosing not to be, which can occur also on a soul level.*
>
> *Now, it's fine to send them prayers, and thoughts of protection, but remember to also trust in the process. Everything has its reason and its timing.*

Easier said than done, though. I remember reading this many years ago, but I didn't believe it was true.

That is often the case. Many people can't accept that free will exists, or if they do, they don't understand exactly what it means for them. This is one of the reasons their lives can become so chaotic and negative.

Remember, it was only when you began to trust that all was as it should be, and to trust your feelings, that things shifted dramatically, and all things that seemed stuck and hopeless moved to another level.

The point here, though, is that it's a lack in trust in the process of the universe that makes us worry about others.

Well, I would also suggest that it's a fear for what would happen to your life if something happened to a loved one. It sounds quite cold when you just quantify it like that.

It may be taken as such, but the basics of life are just that. Choosing to ignore such things does not make them less valid.

If you are in a situation where losing a loved one or something traumatic occurring is going to hurt you, then remember that it's only transcendental. That is, that it fits into a greater plan that you have created for yourself. Though it may be traumatic right now, it will serve you in which direction you are choosing to go.

Not really much comfort for the mother who worries about her children, or the wife who is dependent on her husband for survival. Cold logic doesn't really do much to comfort here.

No, it doesn't. In fact, it's because we have chosen a belief system that has put us into this type of thinking, that we experience such great trauma and suffering. But I put it to you, how do you change anything unless you propose something else? How do you reach another level if you refuse to shift from the one you are at?

What if you not only understood the gifts that lie within every tragedy, but you also never lost touch with those who are departed? What if you could call on them at any time, and feel their strength, energy, and comfort around you? What if they could help you move past the dependence and show you what you are really capable of?

And yet, we resist such a potential reality, because we don't believe, and we don't trust.

It may take a few generations to make this paradigm shift, but only by putting the thought out there, can we make it all happen.

Remedies that work well with Red Chestnut are Gentian, Aspen, Mimulus, and Rock Rose.

Affirmations:

- Those I care about are safe and protected.
- If I need to help someone, I will feel the call and know what to do.
- Everything is in perfect harmony.

26. Rock Rose

Symptoms: Terror and panic. Panic attacks.

Category: Fear

Rock Rose is the remedy for when you are feeling panic or terror.

Generally, it's useful when there is an emergency such as an accident or health issue.

I consider it a more extreme version of the Aspen (anxiety) state of mind. Sometimes vague fears can manifest to a point where there is panic, causing a panic attack. This will stop such an attack.

> *For the empath, especially the psychic empath, there may be periods where they pick up paranormal activity. Perhaps it may be in a house that is haunted, or they sense something nasty around them from an astral level.*

Just to interrupt you here, but are there really such things as hauntings?

> *Everything exists on some level. You can certainly believe that there are places*

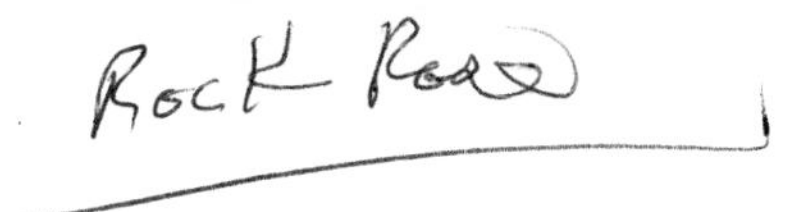

where energies, spirits, echoes, and astral bodies are drawn to. Those who are sensitive will pick them up.

Okay, so ghosts actually exist?

Many are just echoes of energies left behind from the original host. Some are lost or not aware they have died. Some are actual spirits or entities that are either having some fun or are malicious in their intent, as has been discussed in other sections of this document.

You have seen your fair share of spirits.

I don't actually recall anything like that.

Mostly when you were a child. You've heard footsteps walking up and down the hallway at night, seen orbs on your bedroom wall, and there is that hooded apparition that has followed you from place to place.

Actually, I've never seen that. Only others have. I have no clue if it's even real or not.

It's real. Why wouldn't it be? It just can't touch you or go near you. That's all.

Okay, so I guess I would or should be terrified, but to be honest, I've stopped feeling any such things a long time ago.

> *Then you wouldn't need Rock Rose. It is fair to say, though, that many empaths could benefit from it. There are certainly entities that feed on panic and terror, and the empath, being able to pick up on astral bodies and not understanding what they are sensing, may well be spooked about it.*
>
> *Rock Rose helps stop the terror and allows you to face whatever it is that you need to face with calmness and serenity.*
>
> *It's also a good remedy to take when a loved one is in an accident or suddenly gets very sick.*

Update: I eventually discovered that this hooded being was called a *Nobody*. In essence, I believe it's an angelic being that literally has no body and its energy is contained by the cloak. They are considered to be fallen angels.

> *Remedies that work best with Rock Rose are Star of Bethlehem and Mimulus.*

This is one of the five BFR in the Rescue Remedy ™, though it is more effective when taken on its own.

Affirmations:

- I am calm and serene.
- Help is on the way.

27. Rock Water

Symptoms: Self-denial. rigidity. self-repression.

Category: Loneliness / Despondency

Rock Water is the remedy for self-denial and being inflexible.

It is not unusual, as an empath and someone who aspires to be the best they can be, to put very high standards on themselves and their behavior.

What that can lead to is rigid standards and self-denial from the basic joys of life. Sometimes we make sacrifices to get to where we want to be (and sometimes we don't!), but there are some levels where we are denying ourselves things that we could have or do, but choose not to because we believe they are not spiritual or something you should do, or worse, what others feel you shouldn't do.

This can lead to a rigid personality and being uncompromising to what you and others do.

Rock Water will help bring some perspective to things and help you to relax and enjoy what life has to offer.

There are many belief systems that teach us that joy is bad and suffering is good, and that by suffering you are bringing yourself closer to God and that by indulging in enjoyment, you are bringing yourself closer to Satan.

Ironically, likening God to suffering and Satan to joy is the very opposite of what they represent. (Once again, it should be stated that the Biblical Devil is a creation of man, in case my statements are taken as validation.)

There is nothing spiritual about denial of pleasure. There is nothing spiritual about poverty. That is, unless you are wishing to experience your true abundance by experiencing the absence of it.

Being spiritual means being in touch with the soul's aspect of who you really are, and that aspect is light and joy. By denying who you really are, you are diminishing your own light.

This is a common condition of many humans, who have been conditioned to believe that they are not worthy of happiness, nor are they fit to be in the presence of God.

We become less like God and more like our ideas of the Devil with this kind of thinking.

Rock Water helps to free us up and understand that it is not only okay to be a being of light and joy, but it is our birthright.

So, self-denial is not Godly, in other words.

That is what was said.

Remedies that work well with Rock Water are Larch, Crab Apple, and Holly.

Affirmations:

- I am flexible within myself.
- It's okay to indulge myself sometimes.
- I don't need to be rigid in mindset to be perfect.

28. Scleranthus

Symptoms: Inability to choose between alternatives. Attention deficit disorder (ADHD).

Category: Uncertainty

Scleranthus is the remedy for people who have trouble making up their minds. They sway between two extremes. Perhaps one day they will agree to do something, then the next they will have changed their mind, and then later they will change their minds back, and so on.

It may also help with focus and for those with ADHD as it will stop the mind from jumping around and allow it to retain focus.

It may also be useful for those who one day feel they can choose a certain path and the next, become discouraged about it. Then the next day they are back on it. (This can go hand in hand with a Willow (victim) mentality.)

> *This can be an extension of the Centaury Empath, or the Chameleon Empath. They tend to go with whatever thought or presence is in their ear at that moment.*
>
> *Such empaths do not wish to offend anyone and want peace at any price, so they will agree with whatever the prevailing mood*

is and may just as quickly change their mind when the next person walks in, even if it's completely contrary to the previous thoughts.

People refer to them as 'wishy-washy' or 'people pleasers', but the respect for them is very low, as others can clearly see what is going on.

In the end, no one is really happy, and all parties may harbor resentment, especially when, finally alone, the Chameleon Empath states what is really on their mind, which is what neither party wants.

Scleranthus helps clarify what your feelings on a subject really are and aids in helping you to stand by your convictions.

Since this remedy also aids decisions borne of fear and uncertainty, the empath may find this very useful for gaining self-confidence.

It's also a useful remedy for those who are bi-polar. (Which I strongly suspect is a condition empaths suffer from, because they are empaths!)

Scleranthus works well with Centaury, Cerato, and Wild Oats.

Affirmations:

- I am clear on what I should do.
- I am not afraid to state my opinion.
- I am guided on the right path.

29. Star of Bethlehem

Symptoms: shock and trauma. PTSD.

Category: Depression

Star of Bethlehem is the remedy for shock and trauma.

Shock and trauma are very underrated when it comes to the cause of our problems. In my opinion, many empaths are born due to trauma.

> *This is true, as when in the midst of a traumatic event, especially when it's long-term, you begin to put personal safety measures into place. If you feel unsafe, you will learn to pick up on every sign for impending danger or intrusion.*
>
> *In this way, empaths can be born, and it can be due to terrible circumstances, such as child abuse.*
>
> *Empathy can be developed at any point of our lives, but it generally comes into being when we feel the need to have more information than we currently have access to.*

I often suggest people take this remedy a lot. It comes up on a very frequent basis, and when taken can produce life changing results.

Life, in general, tends to bring up traumatic events and many shocks. Accidents, deaths, bad news, break ups, and unexpected events all have their toll on us.

Most of the time we work to get past it, put these things aside, and get on with life. The thing many don't actually realize is that while we bury these events within us, shock and trauma have an accumulative and eventually toxic effect upon our body and psyche.

This can take many years for it to appear, but when it does, it can be finally debilitating and devastating.

One of the results is clinical depression. People often find themselves depressed for no good reason and find that the slightest thing will set them back and send them deeply into a state of depressed agony.

This is different from the Gentian state, where you are discouraged by small setbacks. In this case, setbacks can throw you into a downward spiral.

The bad news is that clinical depression isn't something you can just beat with will power or

just 'get over'. In fact, it's generally very unhelpful to try and do this.

The good news is that taking Star of Bethlehem can completely heal and remove all shock and trauma within you, giving you a new lease of life and making you feel that a tremendous weight has been lifted off your shoulders.

There is a trick to it, however, simple as it may be. The problem with Star of Bethlehem is that it is often overlooked and ignored because it is already part of the Rescue Remedy ™ . Few people realize that its true power is unleashed when it is used by itself.

I've found the best results come when I put two drops directly from the stock bottle on my tongue. There are times when it produces an intense (though for me, not unpleasant) tingling sensation. The stronger it is, the more you need it.

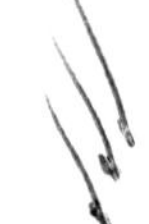

Relief can almost be immediate, though you will have to continue taking the remedy for a few weeks until the healing is complete.

As empaths, this should be in your first aid cabinet. I always have it nearby or carry it with me. I used to suffer from terrible and debilitating depression, and no matter what I tried, I couldn't get over it. I even tried anti-depressants but found they really messed around with my empathy and psychic senses.

Star of Bethlehem cured that for me back in 2002, and I've not suffered any serious depression since then.

If you find you've tried everything, but nothing works for you, I'd highly recommend trying this remedy.

Trauma and shock are an unavoidable part of life, and this is nature's greatest gift, in my opinion.

It's hard to clear trauma as a rule. Doctors will prescribe medication, and the psychiatry industry rakes in billions of dollars from it.

It's the most effective and simplest solution I've found.

This is one of those remedies that prove to me that the BFR's are not a placebo. If they were, then any remedy would have produced the same result. The relief and change in depression levels is profound and tangible. It is also something I have been able to duplicate in others.

The empath is also more susceptible to trauma, as they tend to take things on a much more personal level, and because they are also more open on a psychic level, they are generally more vulnerable.

Being traumatized is also one of the causes of being ungrounded.

Remedies that compliment Star of Bethlehem are Gentian, Larch, and Gorse.

Affirmations:

- All traumas, past and present are clearing.
- I am letting go of the past.

30. Sweet Chestnut

Symptoms: Dark night of the soul. extreme mental anguish. new belief system.

Category: Depression / Despair

Sweet Chestnut is the remedy for letting go of old belief systems and embracing new ones.

The process of accepting a new belief system, which, to some, is also known as 'the dark night of the soul' can be a desolate, painful, and desperately lonely process for those going through it.

Few can really understand the anguish that you are going through, and it may even seem completely trivial to them, but certainly not to you.

For the empath, this state is a nightmare. It's like all things are rushing in towards you and there is no escape. There is no tomorrow, there is no yesterday, there is only a desperate 'now', and you don't see any way out.

And while you may not be suicidal, you also really do no longer wish to be here.

What is happening here is that you are hanging onto an old belief system - one that no longer serves your purpose and one that is holding you back. It's the breaking of old patterns and the parting of old relationships that no longer are healthy for you. It's the acceptance of new beliefs and realities that you may have dismissed as impossible.

It's the holding on, so desperately, to how you think things should be, and the tearing of the energies you are so connected to that creates this intense pain.

This can be due to a marriage breaking up, a change in your lifestyle, departure of a loved one, an acceptance of certain truths about who you really are, or anything that involves a profound change from within.

Sweet Chestnut is the remedy that will gently help you move into a new belief system. It will help you to let go of the past and accept a new future.

It is said, that once we pass through the dark night of the soul, it is the start of real spiritual progress. New possibilities open up to us, and a brighter future awaits.

Sweet Chestnut will help protect you from breaking, bring assurance and relief from where you are, and help you get to where you are going.

I have found it very useful to write down what your current belief system is and look at what no longer serves you or what may be negative to you.

Replacing the ones you no longer need with a positive affirmation, one that reflects what you desire in your life, will produce profound changes in your personal reality.

Be aware, though, that there may be upheaval due to this, as things may need to break and change in order to accommodate those new beliefs.

In the end, you will find things will have improved.

> *One of the reasons why we do enter the dark night of the soul is because we have not accepted that there is much we do not know, or rather, remember. We embrace a belief system, and then hold onto it for dear life and assume that we know all there is to know about things.*
>
> *Remember, though, beliefs create realities, and realities create beliefs, and hence you can become trapped in an unending cycle.*

> *When you have had enough, and have become weary of things not working out*

for you the way you desire them to, you will ask for answers, and they will come.

However, the problem is, you may not listen to what you are being told. You may not accept these new personal truths, and so you ignore them and hang onto what you perceive to be your true reality. Thus entering the Sweet Chestnut state.

Sweet Chestnut is for the changes within and Walnut is for the changes without.

Remedies that work well with Sweet Chestnut are Gorse, Cerato, Walnut, and Wild Oats.

Affirmations:

- I am letting go of beliefs that no longer serve me.
- I am the centre of my reality and control all that happens to me.

31. Vervain

Symptoms: Over-enthusiasm. Overtired. Can't slow down. Obsessive compulsive disorder. Trouble letting go of actions / ideas. Unable to relax.

Category: Controlling others / Exhaustion

Vervain is the remedy for those who are zealous and even fanatical about something. (Much as I am about Bach Flower Remedies at times.)

For the empath, it's when one has an overwhelming desire to help and fix others. And they do this by spreading their philosophies to others like a broken record, taking offence when those others do not seem to listen to their words of wisdom.

It is said that our bad points are our good points turned up a notch too high. By toning them down, you achieve a better balance and are able to give advice as needed, rather than advise that is not wanted.

Vervain is the remedy for those who can't pull back or stop focusing on an idea on an obsessive level.

It's also a useful remedy for those who are trying to get to sleep, but are overly tired or can't seem to settle down after doing an activity that they really enjoyed or worked on.

As an empath, it may be useful for those who feel the pain of others and know the answers, even though others are not ready to accept them. It's all about knowing the timing.

I've found that it is also useful for those who are OCD or have trouble letting go of certain actions or ideas.

This remedy may also help one to relax, especially when they are tense and can't seem to pull back or slow down.

> *Vervain helps the empath when they are just starting out, and they are very enthusiastic about things. It is not uncommon to want to share with all what they are experiencing, which may seem like a miracle for some.*
>
> *However, others may not see things that way, and you may actually drive them away, especially if they feel they have heard it all before.*
>
> *Remember, it's sustained results and demonstration of who you are that really speak volumes in the long run.*

White Chestnut and Vine work well with Vervain.

Affirmations:

- I am relaxed.
- I let go of those thoughts that bind me.
- I am slowing down and letting go.

Symptoms: dominance and inflexibility. controlling others. control freak. Narcissistic. lack of humility. sociopathic tendencies. argumentative.

Category: Controlling others

The Vine type personality may be a nightmare for the empath. Some are hard, dominating, and believe that their way is the only way things should be done.

Others always want to take control, interfere or tell you how to do something. They just can't sit back and let things happen.

Often, they will attempt to take control of a situation that may have little or nothing to do with them.

They are very frustrating to be around as they are always asking why you don't do things another way, or ask why you do things the way that you do?

Often, they are highly intelligent with an ego investment and have narcissistic tendencies.

They have to be the ones in control and refuse to listen to those who may know what is going on or listen to advice.

Such people can be either sociopathic or empathic. Both are certainly possible.

They also tend to be argumentative. Even if you agree with their point of view, they may instantly switch to the opposing one.

They will rarely back you up, even if you're the victim. Sometimes they will do so if they get to show off their knowledge and expertise.

The empath often has trouble coping with those energies and can find themselves stifled and unable to protect themselves against such people. (Walnut and Centaury are the protection remedies for that.)

Vine types can often leave their imprints in their victims, leaving that energy signature to trigger and fester, as to where even years later, it can affect the person.

This is typically done by a parent or a partner who was controlling or abusive.

While giving the Bach Flower Remedy Vine, to the Vine personality, may not always be an option, it's always useful to be aware of these type of people, and how the empath is vulnerable to them.

Taking Vine for those under attack may also help shift that imprint of energy that is stuck within them and that assists in being their own person, in spite of how intense the attacks and beliefs are of the perpetrator.

> *There are definitely Vine type empaths out there. They are empathic to the point where they may use their powers to manipulate the energy of others in order to get their way. They feel their way is the only way, and anyone who goes against them should be cast out or dealt with.*
>
> *You can be sure they are not always pleasant people to those who don't completely agree with them, and can be extremely dangerous, especially to the vulnerable empath.*
>
> *While Vine would certainly help mellow them out and make them more flexible, it is very rare for them to even admit that they would need this remedy, and that they have any issues in the first place.*
>
> *Beware of the Vine type personality. They can be very harmful to your spiritual progress.*
>
> *You can help protect yourself against Vine personalities with Centaury and Walnut.*

Affirmations:

- My way is not the only way.

- I accept that others have their own methods of dealing with things.

- I do not need to control others and I trust in the harmony of things.
- Everything as it's place and time.

Symptoms: Protection from any unwanted influences. The link breaker. external changes. nightmares.

Category: Uncertainty / Easily influenced

Walnut is the remedy for changes that are happening in your life. It is also known as the link breaker when you are trying to break away from someone who seems to hold sway over your emotions.

While Sweet Chestnut is the remedy for changes within, Walnut is the remedy for changes without.

Ideally, it is wonderful for when you are shifting house, starting a new job, going to a new school, or doing something new that takes up a lot of energy and adjusting in your lifestyle.

It's good for culture shock or when you need to adjust to a new lifestyle, time zone or situation.

For the empath, it is also useful when someone is using their influence on you to get what they want.

It may be helpful for those who wish to break up a relationship that has gone bad but cannot seem to bring themselves to do it.

Also, it is useful when you feel someone is psychically attacking you.

I've found that using Walnut and the Bach Flower Remedy Aspen is a good combination for those who have disturbed sleep, such as nightmares, or the sense that they are being attacked on an astral level.

> *Walnut is also a catalyst remedy. When great shifts are needed, it's always worth putting in with whatever remedy mix you're taking. It will not only assist with the change but make the change flow smoother with less trauma or resistance.*

Indeed. I've found that walnut helps prevent system shock, which can occur when changes happen too fast.

> *Walnut can also assist with psychic attacks on any level. It's worth keeping a bottle handy for that. It works well with Mustard.*

> *Remedies that work well with Walnut are Centaury and Sweet Chestnut.*

Affirmations:

- I am adjusting to my current situation.
- All negative links in my life are dissolving.
- You have no power over me.

34. Water Violet

Symptoms: Pride and aloofness. desire to be alone. anti-social. isolation. Elitism. Separation.

Category: Loneliness / Lack of Interest in life

The Water Violet type is often a quiet soul, knowledgeable, but hard to approach or even get hold of, as they have distanced themselves from others.

Success, special knowledge, or special abilities may have caused the person to see himself as separate, possibly better, above, or more knowledgeable then others around them.

For the empath, there is always a danger they may feel that they are a special group of people unto themselves and may not wish to mix with those who are below them in their ignorance and lack of perceptions. Thus, the Water Violet type may shun them and become aloof and full of pride.

Water Violet is the remedy to help bring you back to your oneness and help avoid the desire to separate from others or talk down to them.

It's worth remembering that no one is in your life by chance. All life is experiencing yourself and seeing who you are and are not in others around you.

Writers, gurus, and so-called new-agers may develop Water Violet type personalities. And while they can't answer or be available for everyone, as it's just not humanly possible, Water Violet will help them to remember that we're all in it together.

It's also the remedy for when you don't feel like being around others. This may have nothing to do with your attitude, but more on how you are feeling and if you're up for having company or not.

> *Generally, Water Violet types are very good at what they do, but they often find themselves overwhelmed, too. As a defense measure, they do tend to distance themselves from others.*
>
> *Rather than let others know they can't cope, they tend to become aloof and distant. Water Violet can help them deal with being in demand. Centaury and Willow works well with this remedy in these cases.*

Affirmations:

- I do not mind company.
- I see myself as one with all.

- Everyone has an important part to play in my life.

35. White Chestnut

Symptoms: unwanted thoughts and mental arguments. undesired compulsions or actions. suicidal thoughts and tendencies. trouble sleeping.

Category: Fear / Despondency or Despair / Worry

White Chestnut is the remedy for those who can't shut their mind down, or who can't stop thoughts and mental arguments and chatter.

This often happens when there is something on your mind, such as an argument you've had with someone or maybe worries about keeping a job. It could be a fight with a friend or partner, or maybe you just are running through scenarios in your mind about things that may never happen.

This is especially bothersome when you are trying to get to sleep, and you can't slow your mind down. The same thoughts keep on circling around and around for hours, until you drift off for a short while, and then wake up exhausted.

White Chestnut will help settle those thoughts and help bring perspective.

This is also a very important remedy for those who suffer from suicidal thoughts. They may also have the compulsion to commit suicide and contemplate such things as throwing themselves under a train.

The sufferer might not even be suicidal.

They might also hear tormenting voices in their mind telling them they are no good, not worthy and everyone would be better off without them.

It's vitally important to understand that these are not your own thoughts. They come from another source and are generally external.

Negative entities, demonics or even fallen angelics might be behind these thoughts. I've heard them referred to as *Sorrow Demons.*

White Chestnut will block and protect you against such thoughts. If you know someone who is suicidal, this could save their life.

As a side note, I have seen White Chestnut mixed into Rescue Remedy and marketed as a sleep aid. Personally, I feel that this will not really help as much as just using White Chestnut by itself, or with other remedies, such as Vervain. Rescue Remedy is designed to help people cope with shock, trauma, bad news, and accidents. Adding White Chestnut to the mix just dilutes an already maxed out combination.

This remedy is also useful for those who are trying to still their mind when in meditation.

Also, as empaths, you may tend to worry about certain feelings and energies that you pick up from others. This remedy, when used with Aspen, can bring much needed relief.

White Chestnut works well with Willow, Wild Rose, Gentian, Vervain and Mimulus.

Affirmations:

- My thoughts are my own.
- I have no need to worry.
- I am protected against any malicious intent or entity.
- My mind is at peace.

36. Wild Oat

Symptoms: Uncertainty over one's direction in life. clearing ones path. clearing blocked destinies.

Category: Uncertainty

Wild Oat is the remedy for clarifying which direction to take.

Traditionally, this is a useful remedy for someone who is good at so many things that they don't know what they should be doing. I've found that it can also help when you are unsure what you should actually be doing.

Many empaths seem to be good at doing many things. I feel this is partly from them being able to pick up so much knowledge and information from around them, and from being able to process it into something useful.

It's not unusual for the empath to be stuck about what they really should be doing.

I remember when I first took it in 1985, and after three days I suddenly knew that I wanted to be a healer, something that I have pursued since.

I believe that when you are unsure what your next move should be, taking this remedy will certainly help clarify that.

This remedy is also useful for those who feel their path is blocked by either a curse, psychic attack or the lines of your fate have been messed with.

These things are very real and used to stop people from succeeding on their chosen path. Wild Oats will override such attacks. Lightworkers and those working for the good of this world should take this from time to time.

> *Empaths may also pick up a lot of contradictory feelings and energies, and be uncertain of what choices to make. This is a good remedy to take with Cerato, which helps clarify intuition.*

Affirmations:

- My path is clear.
- I know which direction I should go.
- Nothing can block me.

37. Wild Rose

Symptoms: drifting. resignation. apathy. heaviness of limbs. being drained by others. physical fatigue.

Category: Lack of Interest in life

Wild Rose is the remedy for apathy.

For the empath, apathy can be a major problem not only on a mental level, but also on a physical level. We may find a heaviness of limbs and a complete lack of desire to be able to do anything, or even want to do anything. Unlike Hornbeam, where one is suffering from boredom or lack of motivation but really does have the energy, the Wild Rose type has no energy and every movement and thought is an extreme effort.

I noticed once that after I took Wild Rose, the heaviness in my limbs quickly vanished, and I was able to get on with doing what I was doing, which was having a family Christmas dinner.

The biggest barrier to taking this remedy is that if it's not handed to you, or within reach, you may put off taking it until a more convenient time or until you have the energy to take it.

If you find that you're the type who suffers from this type of malady, you may want to keep a bottle within easy access. Taking this remedy is the hardest part.

This is also a very useful remedy to protect against psychic vampires, or those who hook into your energies and drain you. The Healing Empath is very vulnerable to such things and so will benefit greatly from taking it.

> *It's also worth noting that when an empath is under psychic attack, they can be drained of their will and desire to do things. This remedy helps when you simply can't be bothered doing something you really want to do.*
>
> *It's also useful for the empath that has tried so hard to fit in and act in accordance to society's standards that they no longer have the will to continue on.*
>
> *If you feel drained of energy, Wild Rose can certainly help not only restore the sense of vitality in you, but give you a new lease on life.*
>
> *Wild Rose works well with White Chestnut, Gorse, Olive, Hornbeam, and Oak.*

Affirmations:

- I feel energized.

- Any negative energy hooks in me are now removed.
- I have he energy to do what I desire.

38. Willow

Symptoms: Self-pity and resentment. bitterness. victimhood. self-defeating. blaming others. feelings of injustice or unfairness. Suicidal tendencies.

Category: Depression / Loneliness / Fear

Willow is the remedy for those who feel like they are a victim of circumstances. They may blame others for their misfortunes or feel that life has just dealt them a poor hand.

Also it helps for those who feel life is unfair or justice has not been served.

It also may help with psychic attacks, when, along with tormenting thoughts, negative entities will also magnify the Willow state.

This is another remedy that might well prevent suicide.

Willow is the last of the Bach Flower Remedies. It is also one of the remedies that comes up a lot.

The Willow type is one who is constantly blaming others for their problems, is bitter, resentful, and believes that they are a victim.

Taking Willow helps people to gain a different perspective, understand why things are happening, and what is really going on.

This remedy helps the person to take responsibility for their own choices and reality, and it has wisely been said that it's not until you take responsibility for all of it that you can begin to change any of it.

For those who believe in the concepts of everything being one and of free will, then this remedy will certainly help for when things seem to be spiralling out of control, and you appear helpless in a sea of others machinations.

> *There is something seductive about being a victim. It's you against a harsh, uncaring world that does not understand nor support who you are. It's not unusual for people to want to be angry and actually create situations that will highlight the fact that they are being hard done by.*
>
> *For instance, they may perceive an injustice has been done, but will keep silent about it, hoping others will notice, but also seeing themselves as a victim at the same time. The problem with this type of thinking is that others rarely will see it that way, or if they do, there is a very limited window to get the point across before they expect you to do something or get over it.*
>
> *Being a victim to prove a point, or to highlight just how bad your life is, is generally unproductive. All you are doing is creating a*

poor me drama that no one wishes to be a part of.

Ironically, this type of drama perpetuates the Willow state, as things really will start to look as though you are being the victim.

Generally, there is very little gain in this technique. Being a victim is not only self-destructive, but also stating to the universe that you have given your free will over to others, and that you are choosing what they want rather than what you desire.

Beware of the victim / poor me dramas. You rarely ever gain anything positive from them.

Willow does help bring it back to perspective and help restore your power and balance.

Willow works well with White Chestnut, Holly and Sweet Chestnut.

Affirmations:

- I take responsibility for my own life and reality.
- I release all blame and victimhood I am carrying.
- I am protected against negative feelings from within and from without.

Rescue Remedy ™

The most famous of the Bach Flower Remedies is called The Rescue Remedy ™. It's what is mostly seen at health food stores and pharmacies. As that name is trademarked, it is also referred to as the Five Flower Formula.

It's also what many use as a benchmark for whether the remedies actually work or not.

Studies have been done on this product and the conclusions are generally that it is a placebo.

The problem with such studies is that those conducting the trials didn't have a clue what they were doing.

Rescue Remedy is an emergency formula, so unless the circumstances are right, there simply would be no real benefit.

What does it actually do?

But why is this? In order to understand, let's take a look at what makes up the Rescue Remedy ™.

Star of Bethlehem

This is one of the most important components of this mix. Ironically, it suffers because it's part of it.

This is the remedy for clearing shock and trauma. When taken on its own, it can work miracles. I've seen it cure clinical depression literally overnight.

The problem is, it must be taken by itself for the full effects to be felt.

In this mix it's useful for when you've had an accident, a shock or bad news.

Rock Rose

This will stop or reduce fear and terror. It's wonderful for panic attacks, which is why it will help when you're freaking out over exams.

Its part in this mix is to help calm people who are in a terrible and stressful situation, like a loved one being hurt in a car accident.

Impatiens

This is the only remedy that actually heals what it sounds like: Impatience. Generally said to be for people who are quick thinkers or become irritable when others can't keep up, it's also for when you become angry with yourself for not being fast enough, good enough or deft enough to do something.

Its role in the mix is for calming people down when they are waiting for help to arrive, such as an ambulance.

Clematis

For those who are dreamy or feeling spacey. It is said to help bring one back down to earth. It's actually quite useful for when you feel ungrounded, because it helps pull you back into your body.

Its role in the Rescue Remedy is to help revive those who have fainted or fallen unconscious.

Cherry Plum
For fear of letting go. It's when you hold your emotions so tightly within you, you become afraid of what will happen if you let them out. It's actually the remedy for rage and bitterness expressed. (Willow can help with the internal feeling of bitterness.)

In the Rescue Remedy ™ mix, its use is for when someone is dangerously volatile, exploding or close to doing so.

So now we understand what each remedy does and how they will help in emergency situations.

Taking it for something like anxiety or exhaustion will not do anything as they don't directly address those issues.

Rescue Remedy ™ is an emergency formula and should be used as such. It should be kept in the glovebox of your car and in the first aid kit for times when there has been an accident, bad news or such.

If you are doing general healing, it is best to choose the specific remedy you need in order to gain maximum benefit.

The remedy mix limit is said to be seven, but I feel even that is way too high. Four is optimum and only if those four addresses the specific situation in question.

Rescue Cream ™

This is the Rescue Remedy in a cream-based form, except it also has the added remedy of Crab Apple, which is the cleansing remedy.

The cream itself is remarkable and does an amazing job for healing burns. It helps to sooth rashes, etc. I've sent this cream to some, who use it on their feet after a harsh days work, and find it's the only thing that keeps them going. Some use it as a moisturizer and report great results.

To me, though, its ability to heal burns quickly, remove the pain, and even prevent scarring is one of the most amazing things about this cream. It also provides physical proof that they are not just a placebo.

References:

I acknowledge and am grateful for the following resources that have helped me in writing this book.

Bach Flower Therapy: Theory and Practice by Mechthild Scheffer

Conversations with God series – Neale Donald Walsch

Further resources:

The Empath Resource and Community Website. Created to help empaths connect with each other and host all the various bits and pieces out there. http://empathsupport.com

You can also find an abundance of information and one to one help at my psychic support blog. https://psychicsupport.net

Contacting the Author

I hope you have enjoyed this document. If you did, or even if you didn't, or you have experiences that differ to what has been written here, then please feel free to contact me. I do try to answer all e-mails.

gary@empathsupport.com

Thank you for reading.

Quick summary

The following is a quick summary of the main points of the signs of being an empath. If you are looking for answers quickly, you might find them here.

For more information on the subject, go to the topic in question.

Losing your sense of self and dealing with negative entities.

- An empath can lose their sense of self in other people, world events, or strong energies.
- They may absorb negative energies like a sponge absorbs water and dirt.
- Astral entities may feed off the negative energy of the empath.
- Sending thoughts of love, joy, and light helps protect you against such beings.

Sensitivity to light and noise.

- An empath is more sensitive to light and noise when they are exhausted.
- Their personal space will expand past their normal boundaries.
- They may also pick up smells from astral levels.

- Smells may indicate the presence of other beings being around you.

Sensitivity to Crowds and Parties.

- An empath may struggle to be comfortable if they don't feel they belong or fit in.
- One of the keys to being grounded is self-confidence.
- Physical activity can help ground you.

Anxiety

- Empaths tend to feel anxious without knowing why.
- This may be due to a lack of faith that all is as it should be.
- They also may be picking up feelings from others.
- Worrying about another person can make them feel worried, too.
- If someone needs your help, you will feel their soul call.

- Good communication is important to stop empathic couples from going into a downward spiral of drama and anxiety.
- Set your boundaries and stay within them.

Setting Boundaries

- Boundaries are limits you set for yourself that you do not allow others to go past.
- People love to push others' boundaries, but you may not be doing yourself or the other a favour by indulging them.
- An empath can not only receive feelings, but send them as well, and affect others in a positive or negative way.

Clinical Depression.

- Empaths tend to be prone to clinical depression or depression in general.
- It is not possible to overcome with just will power.
- The causes should be looked at and dealt with.
- Shock and trauma over a long time may lead to clinical depression.

- Empaths tend to make things worse by ignoring events as they happen, and this creates an accumulation of trauma.
- Bach Flower Remedy Star of Bethlehem clears shock and trauma.

Guilt

- Empaths suffer quite a lot from guilt.
- They take on guilt that they are not responsible for.
- Guilt can bring lives to a standstill and lead to depression or even suicide.
- You cannot control how others react. Only how you react. As long as what you have done is with the best intention, then the rest is up to the other parties.
- Pine is the remedy for clearing guilt.

The Levels of Empathy.

- Some empaths can be termed as high level. This refers to their level of awareness and attunement more than any position.

- Being an empath does not mean you can see the future, though many psychics are empathic.

Over sensitivity

- An empath may be very sensitive to how others feel. If they feel others don't want them around, they will remove themselves.
- They will often assume that any negative energy is because of something they have done and will blame themselves for it.
- This can lead to depression.
- It is important for the empath not to compromise themselves by trying to fit in and not change for others.

Being ungrounded

- An empath may become ungrounded if they do not wish to be here.
- This can be due to shock, trauma, fears, etc.
- Self-confidence is one of the main keys to grounding.

Picking up on other people's feelings.

- An empath can pick up on how other people feel.
- It is a good practice to only connect momentarily if you wish to check on someone.
- This can also be useful for seeing if someone is being truthful or not.

Giving others the benefit of the doubt

- An empath has a tendency to always give others the benefit of the doubt.
- People tend to abuse this and use the empath.
- We should take responsibility for when to say 'no' to someone.
- An empath may be reluctant to say 'no' because they fear confrontation and loss.

Strong connection to nature and animals

- Empaths often feel a stronger connection to nature and animals.
- One who is in tune with nature can gain much wisdom.
- An empath can sense if an area is healthy to be around or not and base their

decisions when doing such activities as house hunting, etc.

- Empaths can clear or transmute negative energy to positive energy.
- When clearing energy, it's important to be without expectations as this can produce undesired outcomes.

Feeling the pain and suffering of others

- Empaths often feel the pain and suffering of others.
- Some empaths are like chameleons and change according to the people around them.
- Empaths generally hate to see others suffer.
- Some empaths may feel sympathy pains.
- Sympathy pains can also be a warning that there is an energy blockage within the empath's body.
- An Empath can also match their energies with another, and take on their condition. An empath who is skilled in healing can heal others by healing themselves.

Desire to help others

- Empaths often have an overwhelming desire to help others.
- Unless one is called to do so, the empath should not try and ‘fix’ someone without their permission.
- Empaths often receive soul calls, which is a call for help from one soul to another.

Ability to sense lies and deception

- Empaths have a built-in lie detector.
- They can often sense when something is going on behind their backs.
- They may feel anxiety for no apparent reason.
- Using the ‘twenty questions’ technique, they can generally work out where the source is coming from.
- It is important not to be attached to any outcomes.
- If a person believes what they are saying is true, then the empath will also pick that up as truth, even if it’s not accurate.
- Feelings can change on a moment-to-moment basis, so what you feel is true today, may not be so tomorrow.

Ability to heal others

- High level Empaths tend to be natural healers.
- They can heal remotely. Distance is often no barrier.
- Unless the subject is ready to heal, any healing will be of a temporary nature.

Not feeling like you belong

- Some empaths feel like they don't belong in this world.
- This may be due to different perspectives from those around them, or that they feel separated from everyone.

Feeling overwhelmed

- An empath can often feel overwhelmed with too much energy and become overloaded.
- This is due to absorbing too much negative energies.
- Water is a good cleanser though there are other methods, too.

Being a highly sensitive person

- Empaths can detect even small changes in energies.
- This may be in regard to someone's attitude changing or a situation having new factors in it.
- It is important for the empath not to automatically assume it's because of something they have done.

Buzzing in the ears.

- Some empaths may hear a buzzing or distortion in their ears.
- This may be due to someone trying to communicate with them from another level.
- Many empaths may have other psychic abilities.
- Such abilities can often be enhanced by being an empath.

Changing the energy

- Empaths can empower other people to feel better.

- Sending positive energies to trouble spots can make a dramatic difference.
- Bless your enemies rather than damn them.

Energizing food

- Food and drink can be blessed and energized to help remove negative energies and instill positive ones in it.
- It's best to avoid junk food as the energy is not in harmony with what we need.
- The empath can sense if food is good for them or not.

Someone has to take.

- In order for someone to give, someone has to first take.
- It's best to allow a flow of energy exchange when working with other people.
- There is no shame in letting someone give to you.

Putting your needs last.

- Many empaths have a tendency to put themselves last, leading to exhaustion and burnout.
- It is advisable to set boundaries on your time usage and stick to it.

Shyness

- Many young empaths suffer from being shy.
- This is due to a lack of self-confidence.
- Be who you wish to be in the moment and trust in your feelings.

Chemical imbalances

- Food plays a large part in how we feel.
- Fear and stress may cause chemical imbalances.
- Finding the cause of the imbalance and treating it is important. Also changing your lifestyle may assist.

Dealing with sociopaths

- Sociopaths have little empathy. They don't send as much information out, so an empath will not pick up as much.
- They serve a purpose in our lives, and when that is done, it's time to move on.

- We are here of our own choice, so when we are ready, we can choose a new reality without the sociopath in it.

Narcissists

- A narcissist may also be an empath
- They may be borne due to lack of attention, love or trauma.
- If they are important to you, give them what they need so they can be receptive to healing.
- If they are toxic or destructive, then break ties with them as soon as you can.

Using drugs and alcohol

- Empaths use drugs and alcohol to avoid the pain they feel.
- This can make things worse for them in the long run as it may force the soul out of the body, leaving them more vulnerable to the energies out there.

War and the empath.

- War causes trauma to both the land and the people in it.
- The trauma may cause your chakras to become stuck wide open, and leave you

feeling traumatized and frozen by the feelings.

- Bach Flower Remedies can help.
- It is wise to resolve any conflicts you have in this life because they will just return to plague you at a later time.

Death and the Empath

- Death can be traumatic for the empathy because their energies may still be mixed with the departed.
- Empaths may feel somehow responsible and question "what if" and "why"?
- Funerals are difficult for empaths because they feel so much the grief.
- Loved ones never truly leave.

Vibrational theory

- Everything is vibration, even thoughts and emotions.
- Land and places have their own vibrations.
- Empaths are strongly connected to the vibrations of family members and partners, both positive and negative.
- Vibrations of colors, clothing, gemstones, flower remedies, and meditation can be very helpful in healing.

Soul calls

- A soul call is a cry for help from one soul to another, and can feel irresistible to the empathy.
- Soul calls may be brief or last years.
- Sometimes an empath will need to break the soul connection.

Bach Flower Remedies for Empaths

- Bach Flower Remedies are the vibrational essence of the plant, tree, or even rock.
- They are non-addictive and non-toxic.
- They work at the vibrational level to heal.

Made in the USA
San Bernardino, CA
24 March 2019